BAR
BE
CUE

STÉPHANE REYNAUD'S

BARBECUE

PHOTOGRAPHY BY MARIE-PIERRE MOREL
ILLUSTRATIONS BY JOSÉ REIS DE MATOS

MURDOCH BOOKS

ODE TO THE BARBECUE

The time has come when the sun scorches like embers red with desire, the time has come when the kitchen calls us outside, the time has come to barbecue. The toes have found their cruising speed—spreadout; the body has found its favourite position—stretched out; and the head its preferred state—empty. Spring lays its cards on the table. We want to live outside, we want to eat outside, we want to cook outside. No more gurgling casseroles and misted window panes. The table calls for friends to be gathered around it, the ice cubes tinkle madly, the forecast is fine! You lift up the dust-covered tarpaulin in the backyard, move aside the three bikes, still spattered with mud, so that you can finally reach the must-have accessory of the moment: the BARBECUE. You hasten to clean the grill discreetly, away from prying eyes, the culinary vestiges from the previous year still being clear and present. You empty out what's left of the ashes and a few rusty beer bottle caps jog your memory. You rub the outside of the barbecue with a damp cloth to bring back some sheen to your grilling companion. It's beautiful, almost like new, ready to throw your future table guests into a panic with its benevolent plumes of smoke—because the barbecue has the inexplicable peculiarity of always sighing over that day's assembled guests, whatever the direction of the wind. It clings to the little clothing you're wearing, imprinting its smell upon them, and gets under your skin!

ODE TO THE
BAR
BE
CUE

TABLE OF CONTENTS

6
CONTENTS

8 INTRODUCTION
EQUIPMENT & SAUCES

28 SKEWERS

72 YAKITORI

78 SAUSAGES

92 FILLETS & ROASTS

128 BURGERS

138 RIBS & CUTLETS

154 BARBECUE XXL

166 HIGH & LOW TIDE

202 SHELLFISH HUNT

210 THE BITS ON THE SIDE

244 BLOOPERS AND
DIY BARBECUE

251 INDEX

WHAT TO CHOOSE?

Choosing a barbecue can sometimes be like a Chinese puzzle: electric, gas, wood, with hotplate, rotisserie… What to choose? It's essential first of all to picture the site where your future culinary jousts will take place, so that you can secure the perimeter. This is not the place to cut corners—we don't want to send the neighbourhood up in flames! A barbecue needs to be in an isolated spot without too much vegetation around it, and preferably close to a source of water.

THE ELECTRIC BARBECUE

Often small in size, the electric barbecue has a home on accommodating balconies. It is generally not high-powered and doesn't give a good sear to items like beef rib roasts. On the other hand, it fosters good neighbourly relations in virtue of its being practically smokeless. A water trough under the elements catches grease and prevents it catching alight: the sausages give thanks, the sardines let out a phew of relief! It is perfect for the food-loving couple and is easily transportable. Second, third, fourth floor, long live the electric barbecue!

THE GAS BARBECUE

The gas barbecue has earned its stripes in the eyes of lovers of all forms of grilling. Warning: when bringing the barbecue out of hibernation, it is essential to check the hose connecting the gas cylinder to the barbecue. Rub the connections with soapy water. If any bubbles appear: STOP. You need to change the hose. If the flame is small and yellow, it might be that your gas jets are blocked; turn everything off and wash with lots of water. Once these precautions have been taken, a gas barbecue is easy to use: you light a spark, open up the gas, and away you go. Gas barbecues sometime contain volcanic rocks that are heated by the gas and distribute the heat evenly. They let you sear foods well while managing the heat easily. Gas barbecues are often the most complete in terms of accessories—a cover to create an oven with a temperature control, rotisserie, smoke box, side gas burner, adjustable hotplate…

THE WOOD-FIRED BARBECUE

The wood-fired barbecue is undoubtedly the one most prized by connoisseurs for the superb flavour it gives to food. Its use requires much more thoughtful management, the embers don't happen in the blink of an eye and controlling the temperature and flames can also present a handicap. We all have a memory of sausages that were simultaneously burnt and not cooked, singed and bitter from a fat fire… But we also all have the memory of the beef rib cutlet that was perfectly caramelised on the outside and juicy inside, determined to convert the most vegetarian of vegetarians. The wood-fired barbecue offers the luxury of choosing between a multitude of fuels—pine cones, vine shoots, pine needles, tree wood (yes, it exists!)—according to what's being cooked (ask my friend, he will tell you that duck breasts can only be cooked over vine shoots lit with the rugby pages of a newspaper). A wood-fired barbecue nevertheless presents environmental hazards: a gust of wind, a flying ember, and 10 hectares go up in smoke!

THE BARBECUE HOTPLATE

The barbecue hotplate is the first cousin of the barbecue grill. It allows for almost the same cooking styles as the grill, with the exception of that much sought-after touch of smokiness and char.

The major advantage of the hotplate is that it offers the possibility of cooking several items at the same time with only a little fat—get thee behind me, cholesterol! You take a recipe, combine the ingredients and cook everything together. Sauces and marinades can be added directly without disappearing through a barbecue grill. A hotplate can be bought as a stand-alone appliance or as a barbecue attachment. Like barbecues, both electric and gas hotplates are available. The most important thing is to check how much power the hotplate has so that you can get a good sear on the food. It needs to heat to at least 250°C (500°F), or else forget it!

The coating is also something to consider when choosing your hotplate. Stainless steel is easy to maintain but offers less heat transfer than cast-iron, which is not as easy to maintain. After each use, rub the plate while it's still hot with vinegar and water (this will remove the food tastes) using a metal scraper. Then apply a thin coat of oil (this will prevent the oxidisation of cast-iron hotplates).

IDEAL FOR
ONIONS
SQUID
MUSHROOMS
TOMATOES
CHOPPED VEGETABLES
MARINADES

GEAR

When you're talking barbecue, you're talking special equipment. The barbecue specialist does not tolerate amateurism.

- A longer fork, used to avoid a depilatory episode giving you an arm like a Tour de France cyclist. It is made from rigid steel in order to stand up to the 1.8 kg (4 lb) beef rib cutlet.
- A pair of tongs of substantial length, for easy turning of tumultuous sausages.
- A steel brush, for scrubbing the grill while it still glows with shame.
- An appropriate small stainless-steel case, for holding all the essentials, like an overnight bag full of make-up, which will consolidate your status as a pro. It's good for showing off and would be a great present for your birthday.

Now you're equipped to grill, brown and sear! The only thing left is to slip on the 'Daddy's a Chef' apron you got on Father's Day, make sure the ice-cube trays are full to overflowing (don't forget to check how much wood or charcoal you have if your barbecue is wood-fired), and slip on your favourite hat.
The embers are smoking, the skewers are marinating, the guests are pouring in…It's cooking as an artform!

MAINTENANCE

The maintenance of the barbecue is as important as the foundation of your relationship, like the cement that holds everything together.
A barbecue party often begins with a sudden awakening: the weather's fine, quick, let's have a barbecue. There's a bustle over the morning coffee, phone calls are made, invitations are sent out, let's eat! Your partner is already busy trying to scour the grill—put away like the last time—with broad strokes of the metal brush in a bubble bath (a mix of soap and vinegar). Meanwhile you ponder.
Your partner jumps in the car to stock a refrigerator that has too much empty space for the expected crowd. You check that the beer is in the fridge. Your partner prepares the salad, sets the table. You try to light the heat beads or get the gas ignited: 'Can you give me a hand? I can't get it to work!'
The guests have arrived, your partner gives the barbecue grill—now hot—another rub, and serves drinks. You drink.
Your partner gives you a nudge: 'You should put the meat on to cook.' You sigh and comply. Your partner checks if the meat is cooked, serves the meat, you savour the results: 'You have to admit, barbecuing is such a social way of eating, and it gives you a rest from the cooking as well.' Your partner clears the table, puts things away, makes the coffee, you bring out more wine. The barbecue will stay outside, flecked with the remains of the day's meal…You don't have the strength to put it away: 'I'm too worn out from cooking all day, I'm going to watch the afternoon game on TV.'

BUILDING A BARBECUE

The fantasy of cooking just anywhere, around a flame, as night falls on a steamy day, the heat of the moment like the thrill of a wedding night, lives inside all of us. We picture ourselves with a stack of wood, a hand-caught trout, a few vegetables gleaned from an abandoned field, a bottle of good red wine at the bottom of the backpack, the wide open spaces, a touch of MacGyver, a Swiss knife in the pocket…

Survivor only exists on television. Saturday adventurers must above all observe very strict rules of safety to avoid the firefighters being called out again. The site needs to be suitable for improvising a barbecue, and during summer in many areas such activities are strictly forbidden. The weather musn't be too dry, there mustn't be any wind, and the area must be completely cleared.

That day's 'Boston Rob' must first of all dig a 20 x 20 cm (8 x 8 inch) trench marking out the area of the barbecue, with rocks arranged in the centre along the trench. The fire must be small, using dry wood.

The trout is cooked old-style, speared like a marshmallow on some green wood, and above all you make sure that the embers are TOTALLY extinguished when you leave to rejoin civilisation. Only then can you say that you've won *Survivor*.

BASTING

Items that need to be cooked for a longer time mustn't dry out from exposure to the prolonged heat of a good set of embers—you need to baste them while cooking. To add flavour to chicken, lamb and roasts, use a bunch of aromatic herbs dipped in olive oil or the marinade of the hour. These herbs need to have some resistance, so it is better to use your choice—or a mixture—of herbs, such as thyme, rosemary, bay leaves, sage…Tie them all together with string, dip the bunch in oil and generously caress the beast so it gives the best of itself.

SALT RUBS

Meat and fish often need special attention before a hot night out. They like being taken care of before getting into the action. Pamper them like your sweetheart on date night, bath salts become massage salts—rub them in to bring out their full intensity. The meat and fish are in for a serious relaxation session for a successful gourmet rendezvous.

SICHUAN SALT

2 tablespoons sea salt
1 tablespoon sichuan peppercorns
1 tablespoon caster (superfine) sugar

Pound everything together roughly in a mortar and pestle. This is a good seasoning for fish. The freshness of the pepper paired with the sugar makes it a rub that's both sharp and sweet.

PROVENÇAL SALT

2 tablespoons sea salt
1 teaspoon dried rosemary
1 tablespoon dried thyme
1 teaspoon ground cardamom

Pound everything together roughly in a mortar and pestle. This one accentuates the flavour of meat and fish and brightens a still-grey sky with the sunshine of cardamom.

CURRY SALT

1 teaspoon curry powder
1 teaspoon fennel seeds
1 teaspoon ground ginger
1 teaspoon coriander seeds
20 cloves
1 dried bird's eye chilli
2 tablespoons sea salt

Pound the spices in a mortar and pestle before combining them with the salt.
Your dishes will come to life with the spices of India.
Lamb and chicken dance in a sari.

SPICY SALT

4 bird's eye chillis
1 teaspoon black peppercorns
1 teaspoon dried parsley
1 teaspoon cumin
2 tablespoons sea salt

Pound the spices in a mortar and pestle before combining them with the salt.
To be used in moderation. A salt that lights your fire…
Use with both meats and fish.

BARBECUE SAUCE AND ITS VARIATIONS

Barbecuing naturally lends a quite distinctive taste to foods. The incomparable aroma of a bunch of vine shoots will take duck breast to another level, the resinous note of pine cones adds freshness to fish, and so on.

We can obviously be content going no further than these small culinary 'bonuses' in our fiery epics, but the barbecue chef will want more, and this is the person we need to make happy, to satisfy, to please.

Sauces and marinades then become the signature of the dish, they elevate it to the pantheon of a collective 'mmmm' and give a personal touch to the flavour of the day. Some meats need to excite our desire before being consumed. They need to tenderise, rest, lounge about in a suitable marinade.

The sensual minglings of such a bath are rediscovered on the plate. The flavours blended beforehand are tattooed onto the heart of the meat when it is cooked. The dish of the day can then be eaten as is, rough and ready, or sauced at leisure after cooking, to smooth over the encounter. Other dishes require a friendly jolt to reveal their full potential, and in these cases the sauce plays the role of detonator. When served with grilled foods, it should take them to the next level without distorting their essence.

The cooked product comes first, the sauce becomes its ally and should also exist in perfect harmony with the dish's accompaniments so as not to run into an unfortunate marriage on the plate.

MAYONNAISE AND ITS VARIATIONS

BASIC

200 ml (7 fl oz/approx ¾ cup) mild vegetable or sunflower oil
1 whole egg
1 tablespoon dijon mustard
1 tablespoon vinegar
salt and pepper

Place all the ingredients in the bowl of a food processor.
Process until you obtain the desired consistency.

COCKTAIL

To the basic recipe, add 1 tablespoon tomato sauce (ketchup)
and 1 teaspoon of cognac.

WHOLEGRAIN MUSTARD

In the basic recipe, replace the traditional mustard with
2 tablespoons wholegrain mustard, add 2 tablespoons olive oil.

GARLIC

To the basic recipe, add 2 garlic cloves, 1 tablespoon olive oil
and 2 tablespoons créme fraiche or Greek yoghurt

HERB

To the basic recipe, add 1 bunch chives, finely snipped,
2 sprigs tarragon, finely chopped and 1 French shallot,
finely chopped.

EMULSION SAUCES

These classics are not made often enough, unfortunately, for fear of finding oneself with a split sauce that will then have to face the snickers of guests. Nevertheless, it's a pleasure to enjoy a juicy rare beef rib cutlet generously coated with béarnaise sauce, and a joy to savour a grilled fish covered in beurre blanc…Jump in, tuck in, you're welcome.

BEURRE BLANC

200 g (7 oz) butter
3 egg yolks
juice of half a lemon
salt and pepper

Melt the butter in a saucepan, keep it at room temperature. Whisk the egg yolks in the top part of a double boiler with 3 tablespoons of cold water, until the mixture is pale and thick. (Important: the temperature mustn't go over 80°C/176°F to prevent cooking the yolks.) Whisking continuously, gradually add the melted butter (discarding any liquid that has separated out), then the lemon juice and season.

HOLLANDAISE

250 g (approx 8 oz) butter
1 French shallot
100 ml (3½ fl oz/approx ½ cup) dry white wine
10 ml (2 teaspoons) white wine vinegar
4 egg yolks
salt and pepper

Melt the butter in a saucepan, keep it at room temperature.
Peel and finely chop the French shallot.
Over medium heat, soften the French shallot in the white wine and vinegar, then allow to reduce until almost dry. Off the heat, add the egg yolks, whisking in the top part of a double boiler until the mixture becomes pale and thick. (Important: the temperature mustn't go over 80°C/176°F to prevent cooking the yolks.) Whisking continuously, gradually add the melted butter (discarding any liquid that has separated out), and season.

BÉARNAISE

250 g (9 oz) butter
2 French shallots
½ bunch tarragon
½ bunch chervil
50 ml (approx 1¾ fl oz/3 tablespoons) dry white wine
30 ml (1 fl oz/approx 2 tablespoons) white wine vinegar
1 teaspoon coarsely ground black pepper
4 egg yolks
salt

Melt the butter in a saucepan, keep it at room temperature. Peel and finely chop the French shallots, chop the herbs. Over medium heat, soften the French shallots in the white wine and vinegar, add the herbs and the pepper then allow to reduce until almost dry. Off the heat, add the egg yolks, whisking them in the top of a double boiler until the mixture becomes pale and thick. (Important: the temperature mustn't go over 80°C/176°F to prevent cooking the yolks.) Whisking continuously, gradually add the melted butter (discarding any liquid that has separated out), and season.

CREAMY SAUCES

Creamy sauces are always a hit with the guests of the day. Their smoothness, indulgence and generosity delight impatient tastebuds. They are a blue-chip, minimum-risk investment for a satisfied table.

PEPPER

1 French shallot
1 tablespoon coarsely ground black pepper
50 ml (approx 1¾ oz/3 tablespoons) cognac
200 ml (7 fl oz/approx ¾ cup) veal stock
200 ml (7 fl oz/approx ¾ cup) cream
salt

Peel and finely chop the French shallot. Toast the pepper in a dry saucepan, flambé with the cognac, add the French shallot, and veal stock, reduce for 5 minutes. Add the cream, reduce until it reaches the desired consistency, then season.

SORREL

1 French shallot
100 ml (3½ fl oz/approx ½ cup) white wine
200 ml (7 fl oz/approx ¾ cup) fish stock
200 ml (7 fl oz/approx ¾ cup) cream
1 bunch sorrel
salt and pepper

Peel and finely chop the French shallot. Put the white wine with the French shallot in a saucepan, reduce until almost dry, add the fish stock and the cream, reduce until it reaches the desired consistency. Finely chop the sorrel, add it to the sauce, cook for 5 minutes then season.

ROQUEFORT

150 g (5½ oz) roquefort cheese
300 ml (10½ fl oz/approx 1¼ cups) cream

Melt the roquefort cheese in the cream. Reduce until it reaches the desired consistency.

SAFFRON

1 garlic clove
1 tablespoon pastis (aniseed flavoured liqueur)
200 ml (7 fl oz/approx ¾ cup) fish stock
200 ml (7 fl oz/approx ¾ cup) cream
1 pinch of saffron
1 tablespoon poppy seeds
salt and pepper

Peel and finely chop the garlic. Put the pastis and garlic in a saucepan, reduce until almost dry. Add the fish stock, cream and saffron, reduce until it reaches the desired consistency. Add the poppy seeds before serving and season.

SK
EW
ERS

DIY SKEWERS

When you're talking barbecue, you're talking skewers, the one is unthinkable without the other. The skewer refers both to the skewer that the foods—meat, fish, crustaceans, fruit—are threaded onto, whether metal or wood…and the food cooked this way! Skewers can be a one-dish meal by alternating vegetables with meat and fish. When dealing with fragile foods, it is essential to push the items close together so they don't disappear when you come to cooking them, swallowed up by hungry embers.

Metal skewers are the preferred choice for more lengthy cooking; they will stand up to the heat. Be careful not to put them directly in your mouth or it's a guaranteed burn. Single-use wooden or bamboo skewers are used for shorter cooking times. To help them stand up to the heat better, soak wooden and bamboo skewers in salted water for 10 minutes before using them.

You can also make your own skewers by using aromatic stems from plants such as lemongrass, rosemary, and licorice. The skewer will then give a distinctive taste to the dish by diffusing its own flavour through the food.

HONEY PORK

With your partner, the sweet tooth

Serves 6
Preparation time 20 minutes
Cooking time 10 minutes over gentle heat

700 g (1 lb 9 oz) pork fillet
2 small, firm zucchinis (courgettes)
Marinade:
3 tablespoons liquid honey
150 ml (5 fl oz/approx ⅔ cup) white port (or dry sherry)
1 teaspoon ground ginger
2 tablespoons sesame seeds
salt and pepper

Cut the pork into 3 cm (1¼ inch) cubes. Cut the zucchini into rounds.
For the marinade, combine the honey with the port, ginger and sesame seeds, season.
Assemble the skewers, alternating the pork with the zucchini (packed close together). Coat generously with marinade.
Cook over a gentle heat for about 10 minutes, dipping regularly in the marinade.

Drink with: fruity white with muscat undertones

PORK WITH DRIED FRUIT

With anyone it reminds you of

Serves 6
Preparation time 10 minutes
Cooking time 10 minutes over gentle heat

700 g (1 lb 9 oz) pork fillet
6 dried figs
12 pitted prunes
12 dried apricots
150 ml (5 fl oz/approx ⅔ cup) olive oil
1 tablespoon herbes de Provençe (usually marjoram, oregano, rosemary, thyme)
salt and pepper

Cut the pork into 3 cm (1¼ inch) cubes. Halve the dried figs and remove the stems. Assemble the skewers, alternating meat and dried fruit. Drizzle with some olive oil, scatter over the herbes de Provençe, season.
Cook over gentle heat for 10 minutes. Be careful not to burn the dried fruit.

Drink with: white with lots of oak on the nose and a hint of apricot

VEAL FILLET WITH STREAKY SPECK

With the in-laws (always needing a good feed)

Serves 6
Preparation time 20 minutes
Marinating time 3 hours
Cooking time 10 minutes over gentle heat

700 g (1 lb 9 oz) veal schnitzels
12 thin slices speck (smoked bacon or ham), cartilage removed
Marinade:
150 ml (5 fl oz/approx ⅔ cup) sesame oil
100 ml (3½ fl oz/approx ½ cup) whisky
1 teaspoon ground bay
1 tablespoon coarsely ground black pepper

Slice the veal into 12 strips the same size as the slices of speck (thin and all the same width). Arrange them in a dish.
For the marinade, combine the sesame oil with the whisky, ground bay and pepper, cover the veal with this mixture.
Cover with plastic wrap and chill for 3 hours.
Place a slice of veal on a slice of speck and twist them.
Thread each twist on a skewer and cook over a gentle barbecue heat for 10 minutes. Since the bacon is already salty, there is no need to add salt.

Drink with: your in-laws of course!

BEEF WITH FIGS AND SAKE

With friends who've just come back from Japan

Serves 6
Preparation time 20 minutes
Cooking time 8 minutes over high heat

600 g (1 lb 5 oz) rump steak
200 ml (7 fl oz/approx ¾ cup) sake
1 teaspoon ground ginger
6 fresh figs
150 g (5½ oz) speck (smoked bacon or ham)
12 bulb spring onions
salt and pepper

Cut the rump steak into square pieces 5 mm (¼ inch) thick. Combine with the sake and ginger. Cut the figs and the speck into slices of the same thickness, cut the bulb spring onions in two. Make up the skewers, starting with half a bulb spring onion, then alternate beef, fig and speck. Finish with another half a bulb spring onion. Grill over high heat for 8 minutes, turning the skewer regularly, then season.

Drink with: the sake your friends brought back for you

STEAK WITH SHISO

With my cousins, being sometimes a little shiso

Serves 6
Preparation time 10 minutes
Cooking time 7–8 minutes over high heat

800 g (1 lb 12 oz) skirt steak
assorted baby shiso leaves (purple mint/perilla)
salt and pepper
Marinade:
1 garlic clove
200 ml (7 fl oz/approx ¾ cup) port
100 ml (3½ fl oz/approx ½ cup) balsamic vinegar
1 tablespoon fresh thyme, chopped finely
2 tablespoons olive oil

Cut the steak into cubes. For the marinade, peel and crush the garlic. Combine the port with the vinegar, add the garlic and thyme, bring to the boil. Reduce by half then add the olive oil. Reserve a little marinade for serving.
Place the steak cubes in the marinade, then thread them on the skewers. Cook 7–8 minutes over high heat depending on how you like your meat cooked, season. Serve scattered with baby shiso and drizzle over a little reserved marinade.

Drink with: powerful and rich Pinot Noir

BEEF AND PRAWNS

With one who prefers fish and another who prefers meat, so they may be reconciled

Serves 6
Preparation time 20 minutes
Marinating time 3 hours
Cooking time 7–8 minutes over high heat

600 g (1 lb 5 oz) rump steak
18 king prawns (jumbo shrimp)
Marinade:
2 garlic cloves
1 tablespoon tomato sauce (ketchup)
3 tablespoons concentrated meat extract (see Note)
1 tablespoon olive oil
1 teaspoon coarsely ground black pepper

Cut the rump steak into square slices, 5 mm (¼ inch) thick. For the marinade, peel the garlic and chop it finely. Combine the garlic with the tomato sauce, meat extract, olive oil and pepper.
Place the steak in the marinade and chill for 3 hours. Cut the prawns in two. Assemble the skewers, alternating prawns and beef, and cook them over high heat for 7–8 minutes.

Note: Bovril is a good meat extract.

Drink with: a winemaker you know

MEATBALLS WITH CORIANDER

With a golfer who has lost his ball

Serves 6
Preparation time 30 minutes
Cooking time 5 minutes over high heat

1 bunch coriander (cilantro)
1 lemongrass stem
2 French shallots
1 garlic clove
2 biscottes (large Melba toasts)
800 g (1 lb 12 oz) minced (ground) beef
2 eggs
salt and pepper

Finely chop the coriander and lemongrass. Peel and finely chop the French shallots and garlic clove. Crush the biscottes to crumbs. Combine the minced beef with the eggs, then add all the other ingredients, season. Roll the meatballs in the palm of your hands to the size of a large ball (approx 3 cm/1¼ inch diameter). Cook the meatballs over high heat according to how you like your meat cooked.

Drink with: anything aniseed-flavoured, of course!!

BEEF WITH APPLES AND SPICES

With mates from the office

Serves 6
Preparation time 5 minutes
Cooking time 10 minutes over high heat

600 g (1 lb 5 oz) rump steak
2 granny smith apples
Marinade:
1 garlic clove
1 orange
1 teaspoon liquid honey
1 pinch ground cinnamon
1 pinch ground cardamom
1 pinch ground chilli
3 tablespoons soy sauce
1 tablespoon Maggi seasoning sauce

Cut the rump steak into square slices 5 mm (¼ inch) thick. For the marinade, peel the garlic and chop it finely. Zest and juice the orange, combine with the honey, spices, soy sauce and Maggi sauce. Reserve some marinade for serving.
Dip the meat in the remaining marinade. Halve the apples, remove the seeds, cut each half into slices the same size as the meat. Thread the meat and apple slices on skewers, grill over high heat for 5 minutes. Serve coated with the reserved marinade.

Drink with: rich red filled with the aroma of smoke and the smell of truffle

ONGLET KEBABS

With a real carnivore

Serves 6
Preparation time 15 minutes
Cooking time 5 to 10 minutes over high heat

800 g (1 lb 12 oz) onglet (hanger/flank steak)
1 smoked duck breast
12 bulb spring onions
24 cherry tomatoes
24 button mushrooms
salt
Chilli oil:
100 ml (3½ fl oz/approx ½ cup) olive oil
1 teaspoon ground piment d'Espelette (or hot paprika)
1 teaspoon sesame seeds
1 teaspoon coarsely ground black pepper

Cut the onglet into 3 cm (1¼ inch) cubes. Remove the fat from the smoked duck breast, slice into 5 mm (¼ inch) thick strips, then into small rectangles. Halve the bulb spring onions. For the chilli oil, combine the olive oil with the chilli, sesame seeds and pepper.
On a skewer, thread half a bulb spring onion, then alternate meat, duck, tomato, mushroom and finish with another half a bulb spring onion. Cook the skewers over high heat for 5–10 minutes, according to how you like your meat cooked. Drizzle with chilli oil, season with salt.

Drink with: gutsy quaffing red

GARLIC AND CHILLI CHICKEN

With a fire-breather

Serves 6
Preparation time 20 minutes
Cooking time 15 minutes over gentle heat

100 ml (3½ fl oz/approx ½ cup) tamarind sauce
1 tablespoon brown sugar
6 free-range chicken breast fillets
6 garlic cloves
3 mild long green chillies
3 mild long red chillies
1 small bird's eye chilli
salt and pepper

Heat the tamarind sauce with the brown sugar. Cut the chicken breasts in three lengthways. Peel and finely chop the garlic. Finely chop the mild red and green chillies as well as the bird's eye chilli. Combine the garlic and chillies. Dip the pieces of chicken breast in the tamarind sauce, thread them on skewers and roll them in the chilli-garlic mixture, pressing it on firmly. Cook the skewers over gentle heat for about 15 minutes, season.

Drink with: cherry-flavoured powerful rosé

PINEAPPLE CHICKEN

With your favourite Caribbean music

Serves 6
Preparation time 20 minutes
Marinating time 24 hours
Cooking time 15 minutes over gentle heat

6 free-range chicken breast fillets
300 ml (10½ fl oz/approx 1¼ cups) coconut cream
1 pinch ground chilli
1 lime
1 ripe pineapple
salt and pepper

Cut the chicken breasts into cubes and place them in the coconut cream with the chilli powder and the zest and juice of the lime. Cover and chill this mixture for 24 hours. Peel the pineapple, remove the 'eyes', cut it into quarters then into pieces the same size as the pieces of chicken. Thread the chicken and the pineapple onto the skewers. Cook over gentle heat for about 15 minutes. Season.

Drink with: icy-cold pineapple punch

BOLLYWOOD

With a student of Asian languages

Serves 6
Preparation time 20 minutes
Marinating time 24 hours
Cooking time 15 minutes over gentle heat

6 free-range chicken breast fillets
Marinade:
2 garlic cloves
50 g (1¾ oz) fresh ginger
½ bunch coriander (cilantro), finely chopped
1 teaspoon ground cumin
½ teaspoon ground turmeric
1 pinch cayenne pepper
1 pinch grated nutmeg
2 small tubs plain yoghurt
1 tablespoon sunflower oil
juice of 1 lemon
½ teaspoon caster (superfine) sugar
1 tablespoon tomato sauce (ketchup)
salt

Cut the chicken breasts into cubes.
For the marinade, peel and finely chop the garlic and ginger. In a mortar and pestle, pound the garlic and ginger to a paste with the coriander, cumin, turmeric, cayenne pepper and nutmeg. Combine this mixture with the yoghurt, add the oil, lemon juice, sugar and tomato sauce, season.
Place the chicken in the marinade, cover and chill for 24 hours. Reserve some marinade for cooking. Thread the chicken onto the skewers. Cook over gentle heat for about 15 minutes. Don't hesitate to add some of the reserved marinade while cooking.

Drink with: dry full-bodied chardonnay

MASSAMAN LAMB

With a loudmouth, to spice up his rants

Serves 6
Preparation time 15 minutes
Cooking time 10 minutes over high heat

800 g (1 lb 12 oz) lamb leg meat
fresh ginger, to serve (optional)
1 teaspoon coriander seeds
1 teaspoon whole cumin seeds
1 teaspoon ground cinnamon
20 cloves
5 dried red chillies
Massaman sauce:
3 garlic cloves, finely chopped
1 French shallot, finely chopped
10 g (¼ oz) fresh ginger, finely chopped
zest of 1 lime
1 teaspoon shrimp paste
oil
250 ml (9 fl oz/1 cup) coconut milk

Cut the lamb leg into 3 cm (1¼ inch) cubes. Thread these onto skewers, with a round of fresh ginger on one end, if desired. In a non-stick frying pan, toast the spices with the chillies and grind them in a mortar and pestle. Sprinkle these spices over the skewers.
For the massaman sauce, place the garlic, French shallot, ginger, kaffir lime zest and shrimp paste in the mortar and pestle and pound until you have a smooth paste. Sauté 1 tablespoon of this mixture in a little oil (keep the rest of the paste for another recipe, it will keep for 2 weeks in the refrigerator). Cook for 3–4 minutes, add the coconut milk, gently simmer for 5 minutes.
Barbecue the lamb skewers for 5–10 minutes according to how you like your meat cooked. Coat with massaman sauce.

Drink with: well-chilled Asian beer – yes, it's strong!

BASIL LAMB

With the friends you met on holidays

Serves 6
Preparation time 15 minutes
Cooking time 10 minutes over high heat

800 g (1 lb 12 oz) lamb leg meat
Provençal salt (see page 18)
Basil oil:
1 bunch basil
1 lemon
1 teaspoon liquid honey
200 ml (7 fl oz/approx ¾ cup) olive oil
1 French shallot

Cut the lamb into 3 cm (1¼ inch) cubes. Thread these onto skewers and rub them with the Provençal salt.
For the basil oil, pick the leaves off the basil, zest and juice the lemon, process with the olive oil and honey. Peel the French shallot, chop it up as finely as possible, add to the basil oil. Barbecue the lamb skewers for 5–10 minutes according to how you like the meat cooked. Coat them with basil oil. Serve the Provençal salt on the side.

Drink with: the little rosé you bought together

LAMB, CUMIN AND ALMONDS

With someone who thinks that cumin goes with nothing

Serves 6
Preparation time 15 minutes
Marinating time 3 hours
Cooking time 10 minutes over high heat

800 g (1 lb 12 oz) lamb leg meat
150 g (5½ oz/1½ cups) flaked almonds
2 tablespoons cumin seeds
Marinade:
2 tablespoons maple syrup
200 ml (7 fl oz/approx ¾ cup) traminer riesling
1 teaspoon coarsely ground black pepper
salt

Cut the lamb into 3 cm (1¼ inch) cubes. Toast the almonds in a non-stick frying pan until they're golden brown.
For the marinade, combine the maple syrup with the wine, add the cubes of lamb, season and allow to marinate for 3 hours.
Thread the lamb onto skewers and roll them in the cumin. Cook over high heat 5–10 minutes depending on how you like the meat cooked. Scatter with flaked almonds.

Drink with: the rest of the traminer riesling

VEAL AND GINGER SKEWERS

With your friends from up the coast

Serves 6
Preparation time 20 minutes
Cooking time 10 minutes over gentle heat

800 g (1 lb 12 oz) veal schnitzels
18 medium mushrooms
100 g (3½ oz) fresh ginger
150 ml (5 fl oz/approx ⅔ cup) vodka
Salt and pepper

Cut the veal schnitzels into small square slices of the same size. Cut the mushrooms into thick slices the same size as the pieces of veal. Peel the ginger, slice it thinly. Assemble the skewers, alternating meat, mushrooms and ginger. Cook for 10 minutes over gentle heat, season. Warm the vodka in a saucepan, flambé, pour the vodka over the skewers.

Drink with: the rest of the vodka over ice, it warms you up!

SNAIL-STYLE SKEWERS

With people who know how to take their time

Serves 6
Preparation time 20 minutes
Cooking time 8–9 minutes over high heat

800 g (1 lb 12 oz) veal schnitzels
2 French shallots
1 bunch dill
1 teaspoon coarsely ground black pepper
Salt
Marinade:
3 tablespoons Savora mustard (or American mustard)
1 tablespoon olive oil
1 tablespoon vodka

Slice the veal schnitzels into 2 cm (¾ inch) thick strips. Peel and finely chop the French shallots, chop the dill. Combine the dill, French shallots and pepper, sprinkle this mixture over the strips of veal, season with salt. Roll up the strips like snails. Thread these snails on skewers.
For the marinade, combine the Savora mustard with the olive oil and vodka, spread this mixture over the skewers. Cook for 3–4 minutes over high heat, turn the skewers over.
Cook for a further 5 minutes.

Note: the barbecue grill needs to be very clean and hot so the mustard doesn't stick.

Drink with: an aromatic white with aromas of apple, acacia and apricot (or the rest of the vodka)

THE CLASSIC: HEART, LIVER, KIDNEY

With your adventurous friend

Serves 6
Preparation time 20 minutes
Cooking time 15 minutes over high heat

1 green capsicum (pepper)
1 red capsicum (pepper)
2 veal kidneys
200 g (7 oz) beef heart
200 g (7 oz) calf's liver
salt and pepper
Marinade:
100 ml (3½ fl oz/approx ½ cup) tawny port
100 ml (3½ fl oz/approx ½ cup) olive oil
1 teaspoon brown sugar

Cut the capsicums into 3 cm (1¼ inch) squares. Peel and trim the fat from the kidneys, cut them into pieces the same size as the pieces of capsicum. Cut up the heart in the same way. Peel the calf's liver and cut up in the same way.
For the marinade, combine the port with the olive oil and brown sugar. Add the meats, mix well.
Assemble the skewers, alternating the meats and differently coloured capsicum. Cook over high heat for about 15 minutes, turning the skewers regularly, season.

Drink with: creamy chablis with citrus on the nose

CHICKEN HEART SKEWERS

With your lover—but watch out, that might change after the skewer

Serves 6
Preparation time 10 minutes
Cooking time 10 minutes over high heat

600 g (1 lb 5 oz) chicken hearts
6 sprigs rosemary
Marinade:
1 teaspoon ground piment d'Espelette (or hot paprika)
1 teaspoon ground turmeric
1 teaspoon coarsely ground black pepper
150 ml (5 fl oz/approx ⅔ cup) olive oil
50 ml (approx 1¾ fl oz/3 tablespoons) rum
2 tablespoons sweet soy sauce

Trim fat from the chicken hearts.
For the marinade, combine the spices with the olive oil, rum, soy sauce. Add the chicken hearts, mix well.
Thread the chicken hearts onto the branches of rosemary and cook them over high heat for 10 minutes. Eat immediately.

Drink with: beaujolais (any kind)

KIDNEYS ON LICORICE

With your best friends

Serves 6
Preparation time 1 hour
Cooking time 10 minutes over high heat

3 pale veal kidneys
24 mushrooms
4 sticks of licorice root
Licorice sauce:
2 sticks of licorice root
500 ml (17 fl oz/2 cups) cream
1 tablespoon sichuan peppercorns
50 ml (approx 1¾ fl oz/3 tablespoons) cognac
150 ml (5 fl oz/approx ⅔ cup) veal stock

Meanwhile, trim the fat from the kidneys, cut them into pieces. Halve the mushrooms. Split the 4 sticks of licorice root into sharp skewers. Assemble on the licorice root skewers, alternating mushrooms and pieces of kidney.
To make the licorice sauce, infuse the 2 sticks of licorice root in the cream, barely simmering, for 30 minutes. Set aside.

Toast the sichuan peppercorns in a dry saucepan, deglaze with cognac, flambé and add the veal stock as well as the licorice-infused cream. Reduce until you obtain a syrupy consistency. Cook the skewers for 10 minutes over high heat, coat them with licorice sauce.

Drink with: your best Bordeaux wine (or Premier grand cru) for the memories

VEAL SWEETBREAD SKEWERS

With special friends

Serves 6
Preparation time 1 hour
Cooking time 10 minutes over gentle heat

600 g (1 lb 5 oz) veal sweetbreads (whole)
500 ml (17 fl oz/2 cups) milk
12 fresh cep mushrooms ('champagne cork' or bouchon)
18 sundried tomatoes in oil
3 slices speck (smoked bacon or ham)
olive oil
salt and pepper

Blanch the sweetbreads in milk, bringing them to a bare simmer for 30 minutes. Peel the sweetbreads, removing any veins that should come away easily. Cut the sweetbreads into 4 cm (1½ inch) cubes. Wipe the cep mushrooms with a damp cloth and cut them in two.
Assemble the skewers, alternating the sundried tomatoes, ceps and sweetbreads. Season. Cook the speck on the barbecue until crispy and crumble it into pieces. Cook the skewers over gentle heat for 10 minutes. Drizzle over some olive oil and scatter with the crumbled speck.

Drink with: aged white burgundy with a clear botrytis influence

PEPPERED CALF'S LIVER

With a connoisseur

Serves 6
Preparation time 15 minutes
Marinating time 1 hour
Cooking time 5–6 minutes over high heat

800 g (1 lb 12 oz) calf's liver
salt and pepper
Marinade:
150 ml (5 fl oz/approx ⅔ cup) olive oil
1 tablespoon very finely chopped rosemary leaves
3 tablespoons white balsamic vinegar
2 tablespoons Baies Rose or pink peppercorns (see Note)

Peel the calf's liver, removing the thin menbrane. Cut into
even 3 cm (1¼ inch) cubes.
For the marinade, combine the olive oil with the rosemary,
balsamic vinegar and pepper berries or peppercorns, add
the liver to this mixture and chill for 1 hour.
Thread the liver onto skewers and season. Cook over high
heat for 5–6 minutes, turning the skewers regularly.

Note: Baies Rose is a small pink berry from Brazil with
a sweet peppery taste.

Drink with: crisp white burdundy with an elegant finish

FISH SKEWERS

It's only one step from land to sea. It's summer, you're h
the waves play in unison, you've just pinched a monkfis
from them, pickpocketed a salmon…
The skewer is in the drink, fishing for compliments, sh
gets pickled, sings the blues, the iodine gets the upper
hand. It's reely good!

ROSEMARY-SKEWERED MONKFISH

With your friend Lolotte

Serves 6
Preparation time 15 minutes
Cooking time 6 minutes over high heat

1.2 kg (2 lb 11 oz) monkfish (or any firm fleshed fish)
6 branches of rosemary
salt and pepper
To drizzle:
3 lemons
100 ml (3½ fl oz/approx ½ cup) olive oil
2 tablespoons glucose

Peel the monkfish and remove the central backbone. Remove any pin bones. Cut the monkfish into pieces of the same size. Whittle the branches of rosemary to a point, skewer the pieces of monkfish, rub with olive oil.
For the drizzle, zest the lemons, remove the skin and pith with a knife and extract the segments. Combine the zest, the lemon segments and the olive oil with the sugar syrup.
Sear the skewers for 3 minutes on each side. Drizzle with the lemon-sugar olive oil, season.

Drink with: sauvignon blanc with a light nose and a hint of herbs (of course!)

MONKFISH AND CHORIZO

With a foodie

Serves 6
Preparation time 15 minutes
Marinating time 3 hours
Cooking time 6 minutes over high heat

1.2 kg (2 lb 11 oz) monkfish (or any firm fleshed fish)
100 g (3½ oz) spicy chorizo sausage
6 bulb spring onions
salt and pepper
Marinade:
1 vanilla bean, split with seeds scraped
250 ml (9 fl oz/1 cup) coconut milk
Lemon olive oil:
100 ml (3½ fl oz/approx ½ cup) olive oil
juice of one lemon

Peel the monkfish and remove the central backbone. Remove any pin bones. Cut the monkfish into pieces of the same size.
For the marinade, add the scraped out vanilla bean and seeds to the coconut milk. Marinate the fish in the coconut milk mixture for 3 hours.
Cut the chorizo into thin slices and cut the bulb spring onions in two. On metal skewers, thread half a bulb spring onion, 1 piece of monkfish, 1 slice of chorizo, then monkfish, chorizo, monkfish, chorizo…Finish with another half a bulb spring onion.
Sear the skewers for 3 minutes on each side. Drizzle with olive oil mixed with lemon juice, season.

Drink with: an obscure white with the essence of spring

SESAME SALMON

With someone whose heart you want to open up!

Serves 6
Preparation time 15 minutes
Cooking time 2 minutes over high heat

1 kg (2 lb 4 oz) fresh salmon
5 tablespoons sesame oil
1 tablespoon pastis (aniseed flavoured liqueur)
50 g (1¾ oz) fresh ginger
1 bunch basil
3 tablespoons sesame seeds

Remove the bones from the salmon and cut it into bite-sized pieces. Combine the sesame oil with the pastis. Brush the salmon pieces with this mixture. Peel the ginger and cut into thin slices. Pick the leaves from the basil. Thread onto small skewers 1 slice of ginger, 1 piece of salmon, 1 basil leaf, then ginger, salmon, basil, salmon, ginger. Roll the skewers in the sesame seeds. Sear 1 minute on each side.

Drink with: a smooth and fruity white with stony citrus nose

LEMON SALMON

With your town friends back in the country

Serves 6
Preparation time 10 minutes
Cooking time 2 minutes over high heat

800 g (1 lb 12 oz) fresh salmon
3 lemons
Marinade:
2 tablespoons honey
4 tablespoons light soy sauce
4 tablespoons lemon juice
1 pinch ground piment d'Espelette (or hot paprika)

Remove the bones from the salmon, cut it into bite-sized cubes. Cut each lemon into 12 segments.
For the marinade, combine all of the marinade ingredients. Reserve some for sauce.
Roll the pieces of salmon in the remaining marinade. Thread 1 lemon segment and 1 piece of salmon onto wooden toothpicks. You should obtain 36 small skewers. Sear 1 minute each side. Coat with reserved marinade.

Drink with: complex white burgundy with intense buttery and melon flavours

OLIVE-BASIL SALMON

With another forty-something (like salmon returning to the source)

Serves 6
Preparation time 20 minutes
Cooking time 5 minutes over high heat

zest of 1 lemon
200 ml (7 fl oz/approx ¾ cup) olive oil
1 salmon fillet
30 pitted black dry-salted olives
12 anchovy fillets in oil, chopped
1 bunch basil, leaves stripped (30 leaves)

Chop the lemon zest and combine it with the olive oil.
Set aside.
Using a long knife, remove the skin from the salmon, remove any bones and cut it into 10 x 2 cm (4 x ¾ inch) strips. Stuff each olive with a piece of anchovy. Roll each olive in a basil leaf, wrap it in a strip of salmon. Skewer with a toothpick or small bamboo skewer to hold it in place. Sear the skewers for 5 minutes on each side. Serve drizzled with the lemon oil.

Drink with: grenache-based blend that is rich and bold

YAKITORI

Yakitori are small Japanese skewers grilled over high heat. Yakitori means 'grilled bird'.

They are not however made up of sparrows, robins or other songbirds, but rather of meat, fish, seafood and vegetables. These little skewers are the ideal complement to a cocktail that goes into overtime.

They are dipped in different sauces, the most well-known being teriyaki sauce, which is used for meat and fish as well as chicken. They are enjoyed in bite-sized serves on small wooden skewers, kushis.

You should allow at least six yakitori per person for a full meal, mixing meats and fish to satisfy everyone's appetite. Yakitori are cooked quickly over high heat so that the food is well seared and the sauce caramelises. Bon appétit!

YAKI
TO
RI

FISH YAKITORI

For 6 yakitori
Preparation time 5 minutes
Cooking time 5 minutes

PRAWNS

6 king prawns (jumbo shrimp)
1 teaspoon fennel seeds
100 ml (3½ fl oz/approx ½ cup) olive oil
100 ml (3½ fl oz/approx ½ cup) soy sauce
1 tablespoon brown sugar

Peel the prawns. Crush the fennel seeds in a mortar and
pestle. Combine all of the ingredients. Dip the prawns into
this mixture, thread them onto skewers, cook 5 minutes.

SALMON

300 g (10½ oz) fresh salmon
½ bunch coriander (cilantro)
1 French shallot
1 lemongrass stem
1 tablespoon tamarind sauce
salt and pepper

Remove the bones and skin of the salmon. Pick the leaves
from the coriander. Peel the French shallot, chop it up finely,
chop the lemongrass. Process everything together and add the
tamarind, season. Shape small sausages of the mixture around
the skewers, cook for 5 minutes.

SCALLOPS

6 scallops
2 tablespoons sweet soy sauce
1 tablespoon poppy seeds
juice of 1 lime

Remove the roe from the scallops (if necessary), coat them
with the sweet soy sauce. Thread the scallops onto the skewers,
cook for 2–3 minutes. Serve with the poppyseeds, drizzle with
lime juice.

HAKE

400 g (14 oz) hake
150 ml (5 fl oz/approx ⅔ cup) soy sauce
1 teaspoon ground cumin
1 teaspoon balsamic vinegar
1 tablespoon molasses

Cut the hake into thick strips and thread these onto skewers.
Combine all remaining ingredients and coat the fish with this
marinade. Cook for 5 minutes.

MEAT YAKITORI

For 6 yakitori

DUCK BREAST

1 duck breast
1 garlic clove
2 tablespoons tomato sauce (ketchup)
2 tablespoons soy sauce
1 tablespoon molasses

Remove the fat from the duck breast and slice into thin strips.
Peel the garlic, chop it finely. Combine all of the ingredients
including the duck strips. Thread the duck strips onto the
skewers, cook for 3 minutes.

BEEF COMTÉ

200 g (7 oz) rump steak
2 tablespoons soy sauce
2 tablespoons Savora mustard (or American mustard)
150 g (5½ oz) comté cheese (or Gruyère)
2 tablespoons sesame seeds

Cut the meat into thin strips, 5 cm (2 inch) wide.
Combine the soy sauce and the Savora mustard, dip the
meat into this mixture. Cut the comté cheese into strips,
thread them lengthways onto the skewers then wind the
beef around the cheese. Sprinkle with sesame seeds. Cook
for 3–4 minutes or until the comté begins to melt.

CHICKEN

2 chicken breast fillets
2 French shallots
½ bunch coriander (cilantro)
2 tablespoons créme fraiche or Greek yoghurt
1 tablespoon olive oil
salt and pepper

Cut the chicken lengthways and thread onto skewers. Peel the
French shallots, chop them finely, chop the coriander.
Combine all the flavouring ingredients with the fromage blanc,
add the olive oil, season. Roll the yakitori in this mixture, cook
for 5 minutes.

VEAL

2 thick veal escalopes
1 tablespoon brown sugar
juice of one lemon
150 ml (5 fl oz/approx ⅔ cup) sweet soy sauce
1 tablespoon tomato sauce (ketchup)
salt and pepper

Cut the escalopes into thick strips and thread them onto
skewers. Combine the remaining ingredients. Dip the
yakitori in the sauce, cook for 5 minutes. Season.

CHAPTER II

SAU
SAG
ES

SAUSAGES

The famous sausage is one of the essentials of the barbecue. It keeps us company from the first glimmers of the embers to the last glimmers of those same embers. Gather round unexpected friends, mates from the office, the rugby team that's invited itself over, and the sausage party is up and running. Be careful.

Beneath its friendly appearance, the sausage demands a special vigilance when it comes to cooking. The coals must be both hot enough to sear the sausages and gentle enough to cook them through. Drops of fat in contact with the embers tend to turn the barbecue into a gigantic bonfire. It is therefore preferable to cook sausages on a grill slightly away from the coals. We all have memories of a pre-match hotdog one afternoon during the rugby championship, containing a sausage that was burned on the outside and raw on the inside!

THE PANORAMA OF SAUSAGES

When you're talking sausages, you're talking vast choice.
There are as many varieties as there are butchers.
In France we have:
- the Strasbourg sausage: smooth texture, red colour.
- the knack: smooth texture, orangey colour.
- the Frankfurt sausage: smooth texture, smoky flavour, orangey colour.
- the Morteau sausage: large smoked sausage, coarse texture, poach before grilling.
- the Montbéliard sausage: smoked, cumin flavour, coarse texture, poach before grilling.
- the Toulouse sausage: large sausage, coarse texture.
- the Lyon cervelas sausage: large sausage, coarse texture, flavoured with truffles and pistachios, poach before grilling.
- the sabodet sausage: large pig's-head sausage, poach before grilling.
- the chipolata sausage: thin sausage often flavoured with herbs, coarse texture.
- the diot sausage: garlic-flavoured sausage from the Savoy, coarse texture.
- the merguez sausage: spicy sausage using beef and mutton, no pork.

Many of these can be found in delicatessens and good food stores.

CHIPO LATA FRANK FURT

HOME-MADE SAUSAGES

You don't need to be a butcher to make the sausage of your choice at home. Forget the equipment (mincer, filler attachments…), use your hands and the deed is done.

Base recipe for 6 sausages
Preparation time 20 minutes
Resting time 24 hours

EXOTIC

1 French shallot
50 g (1¾ oz) fresh ginger
1 bunch coriander (cilantro)
½ bunch tarragon
500 g (1 lb 2 oz) sausagemeat
salt and pepper
caul fat, very well rinsed

Peel the French shallot and the ginger, pick the leaves from the herbs. Chop everything finely, combine it with the sausage mince and season. Shape into sausages with your hands and roll them in the caul fat. Refrigerate for 24 hours before cooking.

GOAT'S CHEESE

1 picodon cheese (goat's milk cheese)
6 sage leaves
20 g (¾ oz/1 tablespoon) blanched almonds
500 g (1 lb 2 oz) sausagemeat
1 tablespoon herbes de Provence (usually marjoram, oregano, rosemary, thyme)
salt and pepper
caul fat, very well rinsed

Finely chop the picodon cheese, sage leaves and almonds. Combine these with the sausage mince, add the herbes de Provence, season. Shape into sausages with your hands and roll them in the caul fat. Refrigerate for 24 hours before cooking.

BACK FROM THE WOODS

150 g (5½ oz) cep mushrooms ('champagne cork' or bouchon)
3 garlic cloves
2 tablespoons olive oil
500 g (1 lb 2 oz) sausagemeat
salt and pepper
caul fat, very well rinsed

Wipe the cep mushrooms to remove any soil (don't wash them). Cut them into 1 cm (½ inch) cubes. Peel and chop the garlic. Sauté the mushrooms in the olive oil for 5 minutes with the garlic. Combine this mixture with the sausage mince and season. Shape into sausages with your hands and roll them in the caul fat. Refrigerate for 24 hours before cooking.

MEDITERRANEAN

2 large onions
30 g (1 oz) black pitted Kalamata olives
50 g (1¾ oz) sundried tomatoes
2 tablespoons olive oil
3 garlic cloves, peeled and chopped finely
1 sprig of fresh thyme, leaves chopped very finely
salt and pepper
500 g (1 lb 2 oz) sausagemeat
caul fat, very well rinsed

Peel the onions and finely chop them. Roughly chop the olives and the sundried tomatoes. In a frying pan, soften the onions in the olive oil, add the olives, garlic, thyme leaves and stew together. Combine this mixture with the sausage mince and season. Shape into sausages with your hands and roll them in the caul fat. Refrigerate for 24 hours before cooking.

CAILLETTES

With two foodies ready to take on your choice of ingredient argument

Serves 6
Preparation time 45 minutes
Cooking time 20 minutes over gentle heat

1 bunch silverbeet (Swiss chard)
4 bulb spring onions
100 ml (3½ fl oz/approx ½ cup) olive oil
salt and pepper
800 g (1 lb 12 oz) sausagemeat
caul fat, very well rinsed

Chop the stem and leaves of the silverbeet as finely as possible.
Chop the bulb spring onions, including the green part.
Gently sauté the silverbeet and spring onions in the olive oil
for 15 minutes. The silverbeet stem should be tender. Cool.
Combine the silverbeet-onion preparation with the sausage
mince, season well. Roll into balls the size of a tennis ball
and wrap them in caul fat. You can make one large caillette
per person or two smaller ones. Refrigerate for 24 hours
before cooking.
Cook over gentle heat for 20 minutes, turning them regularly.

**Drink with: sexy red full of plums, boysenberry and white
pepper aromas**

86
SAUSAGES

SAUSAGE IN THE EMBERS

With a full-blood sausage connoisseur to pay him homage

Serves 6
Preparation time 15 minutes
Cooking time 30 minutes over gentle heat

2 fresh Lyon sausages
2 large slices of speck (smoked ham or bacon)
2 bay leaves
4 cloves
6 garlic cloves, unpeeled
6 French shallots
1 teaspoon quatre-épices (see Note)
400 ml (14 fl oz/approx 1⅔ cup) beaujolais
80 g (2¾ oz) butter

Make two large parcels out of foil, the same length as the sausages. In each of the parcels arrange 1 sausage, 1 slice of speck, 1 bay leaf, 2 cloves, 3 garlic cloves and 3 French shallots. Combine the spices with the beaujolais, divide the wine between the parcels and add half the butter to each. Seal each parcel airtight and place the parcels over gentle heat for 30 minutes. Slice the sausage, accompany each serving with one of the cooked shallots and one of the garlic cloves and coat with the wine sauce from the foil parcels.

Note: quatre-épices literally means four spices and is common in France. It's a mixture of two parts ground white pepper, one part each of ground ginger, ground nutmeg and ground cloves.

Drink with: vibrant ruby red beaujolais (what's left of the above)

CUSTOMISED MERGUEZ

With your friend from the match in memory of that last hotdog you ate at the ground

Serves 6
Preparation time 20 minutes
Cooking time 10 minutes over gentle heat

18 merguez sausages
1 teaspoon ground cinnamon
1 apple
1 orange
caul fat, very well rinsed

Remove the skin from the merguez, work the meat with a fork to loosen the texture, add the cinnamon. Peel the apple and cut into small cubes. Juice and zest the orange, combine with the apples then the merguez meat. Shape mixture into ovals 8 cm (3¼ inch) long, roll them in the caul fat. Refrigerate for 24 hours before cooking.
Cook them over gentle heat for 10 minutes.

Drink with: a good icy-cold beer to commemorate…

CHAPTER III

FILLETS & ROASTS

CHICKEN BREAST WITH COCONUT MILK

With your girlfriend

Serves 6
Preparation time 20 minutes
Resting time 3 hours
Cooking time 5 minutes over high heat

6 free-range chicken breast fillets
2 limes
salt and pepper
Coconut milk marinade:
50 g (1¾ oz) fresh ginger
2 French shallots
2 garlic cloves
2 tablespoons sunflower oil
1 tablespoon sugar
350 ml (approx 12 fl oz/approx 1½ cups)
  coconut milk
1 bunch chives

Slice the chicken breasts into thin strips. Juice and zest
the limes, sprinkle the juice and zest over the chicken.
For the marinade, peel the ginger, French shallots and garlic.
Chop them all up then gently sauté in the oil for 5 minutes,
adding the sugar. Off the heat, pour in the coconut milk.
Snip the chives into 1 cm (½ inch) lengths and add them
to the mixture. Pour this mixture over the chicken and chill
for 3 hours.
Cook the chicken over high heat until well browned.
Serve coated with the rest of the marinade.

**Drink with: gorgeous rosé with the colour of summer
sunset (slightly chilled)**

DUCK TENDERLOINS À L'ORANGE

With mates you want to amaze

Serves 6
Preparation time 15 minutes
Marinating time 3 hours
Cooking time 5 minutes over high heat

800 g (1 lb 12 oz) duck tenderloins or
skinned duck breasts
cut into strips
salt and pepper
Marinade:
2 oranges
150 ml (5 fl oz/approx ⅔ cup) wine vinegar
25 g (1 oz/2 tablespoons) sugar
2 tablespoons Grand Marnier
Orange salad with red onions:
2 oranges
2 red onions
3 spring onions (scallions)
3 tablespoons olive oil

For the marinade, juice and zest the 2 oranges. Heat the
vinegar with the sugar until it caramelises, add the orange juice
and zests, then the Grand Marnier. Cool. Place the duck
tenderloins in this mixture and chill for 3 hours.
For the salad, remove the skin and pith of the 2 oranges to
obtain the segments. Peel and finely chop the red onions, slice
the spring onions thinly. Combine all the salad ingredients
with the olive oil.
Cook the tenderloins for 5 minutes over high heat.
Combine with the orange and red onion salad, season.

Drink with: deep dark purple cabernet with a soft finish

DUCK TENDERLOINS WITH SUMMER VEGETABLES

With people in a hurry

Serves 6
Preparation time 10 minutes
Cooking time 10 minutes on the barbecue hotplate

3 garlic cloves
4 large onions

12 long mild chillies, red and green
3 young zucchinis (courgettes)
600 g (1 lb 5 oz) duck tenderloins or skinned
  duck breasts, cut into strips
1 small jar or can baby corn (unsweetened)
2 tablespoons balsamic vinegar
3 tablespoons soy sauce
olive oil

Peel and finely slice the garlic and onions. Halve the chillies,
remove the seeds. Cut the zucchini into even lengths. Sauté
the onions and garlic on the barbecue hotplate in a little olive
oil, add the duck tenderloins and barbecue 3–4 minutes.
Then add the rest of the vegetables and cook for 5 minutes
more, stirring well. Deglaze with the balsamic vinegar and
soy sauce. Serve immediately.

Drink with: pale and delicate rosé

SWEET-SOUR CHICKEN DRUMSTICKS

With your ex at the end of a bittersweet affair

Serves 6
Preparation time 15 minutes
Cooking time 20 minutes over gentle heat

12 chicken drumsticks
salt
Sweet-sour sauce:
5 garlic cloves
1 red onion
100 g (3½ oz) fresh pineapple
100 g (3½ oz/approx ½ cup) sugar
2 tablespoons rice vinegar
4 tablespoons tomato sauce (ketchup)

For the sauce, peel the garlic and onion, slice them thinly.
Process all of the sauce ingredients together to make a smooth
purée. Cook this preparation over a low heat in a frying pan
for 5 minutes. It should start to caramelise. Season. Set some
of the sauce aside to use for dipping.
Dip the drumsticks in the remainder of the sauce, cook
them over gentle heat for 20 minutes, turning them regularly.
Serve with the reserved sweet-sour sauce.

Drink with: champagne (the real stuff!)

EPIGRAMS OF LAMB WITH TAMARIND

With someone who's not afraid to get their hands dirty

Serves 6
Preparation time 15 minutes
Resting time 3 hours
Cooking time 20 minutes over gentle heat

6 lamb epigrams (boned breast pieces)
Marinade:
4 bulb spring onions
1 tablespoon tamarind paste
3 tablespoons tomato sauce (ketchup)
2 tablespoons sunflower oil
6 tablespoons soy sauce
1 teaspoon ground cumin
1 tablespoon brown sugar
juice of 2 lemons
salt and pepper

For the marinade, finely chop the bulb spring onions. Combine all of the marinade ingredients together to make a smooth mixture. Cover the lamb epigrams with this mixture and chill, covered for 3 hours.
Cook over gentle heat for 20 minutes, turning the epigrams regularly and coating them regularly with marinade.

Drink with: simple rosé blend (with a hint of merlot, perhaps)

RABBIT THIGHS WITH SUNDRIED TOMATOES

With someone who doesn't ask questions

Serves 6
Preparation time 20 minutes
Marinating time 24 hours
Cooking time 30 minutes over gentle heat

6 lovely rabbit thighs
assorted heirloom tomatoes
75 ml (approx 2¼ fl oz/⅓ cup) olive oil
½ tablespoon herbes de Provence (usually marjoram, oregano, rosemary, thyme)
salt and pepper

Marinade:
150 g (5½ oz) sundried tomatoes in oil
2 garlic cloves
½ tablespoon herbes de Provence (usually marjoram, oregano, rosemary, thyme)
10 g (¼ oz) fresh ginger
75 ml (approx 2¼ fl oz/⅓ cup) olive oil

The day before prepare the marinade. Process together the sundried tomatoes, peeled garlic, herbes de Provence, ginger and olive oil until you have a paste. Season. Make a series of regular incisions in the rabbit thighs down to the bone. Fill with the tomato paste, wrap the thighs tightly in plastic wrap and chill for 24 hours.
Cook the rabbit over gentle heat for 15 minutes on each side, turning regularly. Brush the tomatoes with the olive oil, add the herbes de Provence, season. Barbecue the tomatoes for 5 minutes.

Drink with: cabernet with blackberry aroma

BEEF SHOULDER MARINATED IN CANOLA OIL

With a vampire

Serves 6
Preparation time 15 minutes
Marinating 24 hours
Cooking time 3 minutes over high heat

1 kg (2 lb 4 oz) beef shoulder
Marinade:
12 bulb spring onions
1 bunch basil, leaves reserved
2 tablespoons maple syrup
300 ml (10½ fl oz/approx 1¼ cups) canola oil
1 teaspoon tandoori spices
1 teaspoon fennel seeds
juice of one lemon
salt and pepper

Cut the beef into thin slices across the grain of the meat. For the marinade, finely slice the bulb spring onions as well as the basil leaves. Combine all of the marinade ingredients, reserve a little for serving. Cover the beef with the remaining mixture and cover with plastic film. Chill for 24 hours.
Quickly sear the beef shoulder over high heat.
Serve immediately with the reserved marinade.

Drink with: something blood red

BONED SADDLE
OF RABBIT

With your large rabbit because you like him very much

Serves 6
Preparation time 20 minutes
Cooking time 20 minutes over gentle heat

3 saddles of rabbit
caul fat, very well rinsed
salt and pepper
Stuffing:
1 French shallot
1 bunch basil
50 g (1¾ oz) sundried tomatoes in oil
3 artichokes in oil
1 spring onion (scallion)
1 slice of stale sandwich bread

Bone the saddles of rabbit, taking care not to damage the meat.
Lay the saddles out flat, season.
For the stuffing, peel the French shallot, slice it thickly, pick
the leaves from the basil. Process all of the stuffing ingredients
together to make a paste.
Place the stuffing between the loin and the flap of the saddle,
close over the flap, roll in the caul fat. Cook over gentle heat
for 20 minutes turning the rabbit regularly.

Drink with: rich and weighty cabernet sauvignon

PORK FILLETS WITH PISTACHIO PESTO

With your Italian butcher

Serves 6
Preparation time 30 minutes
Cooking time 20 minutes over gentle heat

3 pork fillets
salt and pepper
Pistachio pesto:
1 bunch basil
3 garlic cloves
100 g (3½ oz) good parmesan cheese
1 slice of stale country bread
100 g (3½ oz) shelled pistachios
200 ml (7 fl oz/approx ¾ cup) olive oil

Carefully butterfly the fillets by slicing them lengthways. For the pesto, pick the leaves from the basil. Peel the garlic, cut the parmesan into cubes. Crumble the bread. Process all of the pesto ingredients together to obtain a fairly coarse paste. Season the fillets, fill them with pistachio pesto, roll them back up to enclose the filling. Tie them up with cooking twine soaked in salted water. Cook over gentle heat for 20 minutes, turning them regularly.

Drink with: Italian chianti

LIKE A PAUPIETTE WITH SWEET ONIONS

With the village brass band

Serves 6
Preparation time 40 minutes
Cooking time 10 minutes over gentle heat

6 thin veal schnitzels
Onion confit:
4 onions (mild sweet onions)
2 garlic cloves
50 g (1¾ oz) black olives
1 bunch coriander (cilantro)
1 tablespoon pine nuts
1 tablespoon ground cumin
100 ml (3½ fl oz/approx ½ cup) olive oil
salt and pepper

For the confit, peel the onions and garlic and slice them.
Roughly chop the black olives, pick the leaves from the
coriander and chop them. Gently sauté the onions and garlic
in the olive oil with the black olives, pine nuts, cumin and
coriander for 10 minutes. The onions should stew down.
Season.
Lay out the veal schnitzels and season them. Divide the onion
confit between the six schnitzels, close them up around the
filling like 'paupiettes' and tie them with cooking twine soaked
in salted water. Cook over gentle heat for 10 minutes.

Drink with: viognier with good intensity on the nose

DUCK BREAST & ZUCCHINI TOURNEDOS

With the little one's rugby team

Serves 6
Preparation time 30 minutes
Cooking time 10 minutes over gentle heat

3 duck breasts
3 young zucchini (courgettes)
salt
Cep mushroom powder:
50 g (1¾ oz) dried cep mushrooms ('champagne
   cork' or bouchon) or porcini
2 tablespoons coarsely ground black pepper
1 tablespoon herbes de Provençe (usually
   marjoram, oregano, rosemary, thyme)

For the mushroom powder, process the dried cep mushrooms
until finely ground, combine them with the pepper and herbes
de Provençe.
Cut the duck breasts lengthways into 3 mm (⅛ inch) wide
strips. Lay out the strips of duck two by two on top of each
other, alternating layers of fat and lean. Cut the zucchini into
strips using a vegetable peeler. Lay the strips of zucchini on top
of the duck, season with the mushroom powder and season
with salt. Roll up the strips tightly to make tournedos and tie
with string. Make 6 tournedos in this way. Cook over gentle
heat 5 minutes each side.

**Drink with: cabernet sauvignon and merlot blend
(magnum bottle)**

VEAL ROULADE WITH JAMÓN

With a flamenco dancer

Serves 6
Preparation time 20 minutes
Cooking time 10 minutes over gentle heat

6 thin veal schnitzels
6 slices of jamón Serrano (dry-cured
  Spanish ham)
pepper
Anchovy stuffing:
1 French shallot
12 anchovies in oil
1 bunch tarragon
50 g (1¾ oz) parmesan cheese
100 ml (3½ fl oz/approx ½ cup) olive oil
50 g (1¾ oz/approx ½ cup) shelled walnuts

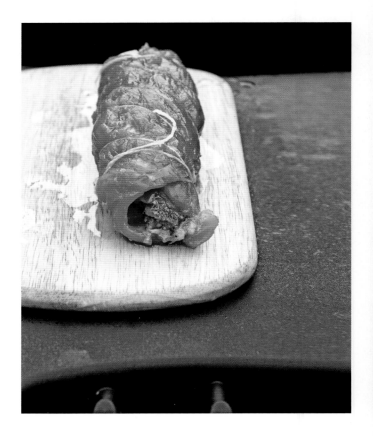

For the stuffing, peel the French shallot, chop it finely.
Roughly chop the anchovies. Process together the tarragon,
parmesan, olive oil and walnuts. Add the pieces of anchovy
and the chopped shallot.
Lay the schnitzels out flat, season them with pepper. Place
a slice of jamón on each schnitzel, then the anchovy mixture.
Roll up the schnitzels and tie them with cooking twine soaked
in salted water. Cook over gentle heat for 10 minutes, turning
the schnitzels regularly.

Drink with: best chardonnay on the shelf

BUTTERFLIED LAMB SHOULDER

With the guests at your anniversary

Serves 6
Preparation time 20 minutes
Cooking time 45 minutes over gentle heat

2 lamb shoulders
salt with Moroccan spices
12 sage leaves
200 ml (7 fl oz/approx ¾ cup) olive oil
1 kg (2 lb 4 oz) eggplants (aubergines)

Bone the lamb shoulders, butterfly them out flat and rub with the spiced salt. Finely slice the sage leaves, combine them with the olive oil, set aside at room temperature. Cut the eggplants into rounds.
Barbecue the lamb shoulders over gentle heat for 45 minutes.
Barbecue the rounds of eggplant for 3–4 minutes.
Serve everything with the sage oil.

Drink with: at least five-year-old red, it's your anniversary after all

PEPPERMINT LAMB LEG STEAK

With a Brit in exile

Serves 6
Preparation time 15 minutes
Cooking time 10 minutes over high heat and on the hotplate

6 lamb leg steaks
Vegetables:
6 garlic cloves
50 g (1¾ oz) fresh ginger
6 French shallots
2 tablespoons olive oil
1 bunch peppermint, leaves torn
salt and pepper

To prepare the vegetables, peel and roughly slice the garlic, ginger and French shallots. Gently sauté the French shallots with the garlic and ginger in the olive oil for 7–8 minutes, add the torn peppermint leaves just before serving, season. Barbecue the lamb steaks over high heat. The cooking time will depend how you like the lamb cooked. Serve with the vegetables.

Drink with: elegant merlot blend with a lingering finish

GARLIC-STUDDED LAMB LEG STEAK

With whoever you like, but not for a tête-à-tête

Serves 6
Preparation time 15 minutes
Cooking time 10 minutes over high heat

12 black Kalamata olives
6 garlic cloves
2 branches of rosemary
12 anchovies in oil
6 lamb leg steaks
pepper

Pit the black olives. Peel and quarter the garlic cloves and remove the sprout in the middle. Cut the rosemary into small tufts.
Cut the anchovies in two.
Make small incisions in the lamb steaks using a pointed knife. Insert garlic, olives, anchovies and rosemary. Cook over high heat for 5 minutes on each side. Season with pepper, place the salt on the table (the anchovies already give quite a salty taste).

Drink with: cabernet merlot with silky tannins

SADDLE OF LAMB

With a delicate cyclist

Serves 6
Preparation time 30 minutes
Cooking time 20 minutes over gentle heat

1 beautiful saddle of lamb
1 bunch basil
2 French shallots
salt and pepper
Garlic-hazelnut purée:
8 garlic cloves
200 ml (7 fl oz/approx ¾ cup) milk
1 tablespoon hazelnuts

Bone the saddle of lamb, separating the two loins.
For the purée, peel the garlic, cook it for 15 minutes
in the milk. Strain and discard the milk. Purée the garlic.
Roughly crush the hazelnuts. Combine the garlic purée
with the hazelnuts.
Pick the leaves from the basil, peel and finely chop the French
shallots. Lay out the two halves of the saddle, skin side down.
Spread the inside with the garlic-hazelnut purée, add the basil
and the finely chopped French shallots and season.
Close the flaps of the saddle over the loin and tie closed
with string. Cook over gentle heat for 20 minutes, turning
the saddle regularly.

**Drink with: an organic wine, it won't leave any traces in the
drug test**

SCHNITZEL AND AGED COMTÉ

With a boxer on the come-back

Serves 6
Preparation time 30 minutes
Cooking time 7–8 minutes over gentle heat

3 veal schnitzels, 1 cm (½ inch) thick
salt
200 g (7 oz) aged Comté cheese (or Gruyére)
caul fat, very well rinsed
Marinade:
1 tablespoon honey
1 tablespoon white port
1 teaspoon sichuan peppercorns
1 tablespoon fennel seeds

For the marinade, combine the honey with the port, pepper and fennel seeds.
Chop the veal escalopes into 1 cm (½ inch) cubes, put them in the marinade and season with salt.
Cut the Comté cheese into cubes the same size as the veal. Thread onto skewers, alternating meat and cheese. Roll each skewer tightly in the caul fat. Cook over gentle heat for 10 minutes, turning the skewers regularly.

Drink with: cool climate white

SPECK

With your old uncle and aunt, who love a bit of pork

Serves 6
Preparation time 10 minutes
Cooking time 10 minutes over gentle heat

2 bulb spring onions
1 baguette
2 garlic cloves
100 ml (3½ fl oz/approx ½ cup) canola oil
6 beautiful fresh tomatoes
1 bunch basil
12 slices of speck (smoked ham or bacon),
  5 mm (¼ inch) thick

Finely slice the bulb spring onions. Cut the baguette into slices lengthways. Peel the garlic and rub it over the slices of bread. Drizzle the baguette with some canola oil. Slice the tomatoes, roughly slice the basil. Barbecue the slices of speck for 5 minutes on each side and toast the slices of baguette. Serve everything tapas-style.

Drink with: well-chilled cask of rosé (they'll be sleeping over anyway)

VEAL FLANK AND SARASSOU

With a seasoned camper who needs new recipes

Serves 6
Preparation time 15 minutes
Cooking time 30 minutes over gentle heat

6 slices of veal flank (or boned breast)
spicy salt (see page 18)
Sarassou:
2 French shallots
1 bunch radishes
1 celery stalk
250 g (9 oz) sarassou or créme fraiche
  or Greek yoghurt
sea salt and coarsely ground black pepper

Remove the cartilage from the veal flank, rub the meat with the spicy salt. Barbecue the veal over gentle heat 15 minutes on each side: they should be nice and brown.
For the sarassou, peel the French shallots and chop them finely. Slice the radishes and celery. Combine all of these with the sarassou, season with sea salt and coarsely ground black pepper. Serve the sarassou over the cooked veal.

Drink with: slam dunk red

SANDWICH-STYLE DUCK BREAST

With Jacky, obviously

Serves 6
Preparation time 15 minutes
Cooking time 15 minutes over gentle heat

1 red onion
150 g (5½ oz) sheep's milk cheese
3 duck breasts
salt and pepper
2 tablespoons tomato sauce (ketchup)

Peel and slice the red onion. Thinly slice the sheep's milk
cheese. Using a sharp knife, slash the skin side of the duck
breasts in a criss-cross pattern. Cut the breasts in two, season.
Place some cheese, onion and tomato sauce on one half,
cover with the other half and tie with cooking twine soaked
in salted water.
Cook over gentle heat, set back so that the fat doesn't catch
alight, 6–7 minutes on each side.

Drink with: cabernet sauvignon and Jacky, obviously

ANDOUILLETTE EN PAPILLOTE

With your local politician (andouillette is like politics, it should smell a bit like sh*t, but not too much)

Serves 6
Preparation time 15 minutes
Cooking time 15 minutes over gentle heat

6 French shallots
6 andouillettes (French sausages)
6 garlic cloves
1 bunch lemon thyme
300 ml (10½ fl oz/approx 1¼ cups) chénas-style beaujolais
300 ml (10½ fl oz/approx 1¼ cups) tawny port
120 g (4¼ oz) butter
salt and pepper

Peel the French shallots. Make parcels out of foil. Place 1 andouillette in each parcel, add 1 unpeeled garlic clove, 1 French shallot and a little lemon thyme. Divide the beaujolais, port and butter between the parcels, season. Seal the parcels airtight, place them over gentle heat for 15 minutes. Serve the parcels on the plate.

Drink with: beaujoulais of breadth and substance (unlike the politician)

BURGERS

The hamburger is no doubt the most global sandwich ever created. Its origins date back to the nineteenth century with the departure of Germans from the port of Hamburg towards a welcoming America. This sandwich, made of cooked minced meat served between two pieces of bread, became the standard dish of these trans-Atlantic crossings. Once in the United States, 'steak cooked Hamburg-style' quickly found a place in the restaurants around New York harbour. It attracted a number of homesick Germans, but also people from all corners of the globe.

The hamburger is born, and starts its international rise. It will first spread throughout the United States, in particular in 1931, with the appearance in the Popeye comics of the character of Wimpy, a true hamburger lover, which gives rise to the idea of a chain of restaurants dedicated to the dish. This enjoys rapid success, competitors rush to follow, the concept of a low price, quickly served meal in itself becoming its hallmark. Its return to Europe in the 1970s marks the conclusion of its epic tale, it is forever lodged in posterity. The hamburger today is synonymous with globalisation.

BBQ
FAST
FOOD

THE TRUE BURGER

The basic components of the hamburger are: minced meat, a soft and slightly sweet bun with sesame seeds, sweet onion, tomato sauce, sweet-sour pickles, slices of cheddar cheese, bacon and lettuce.

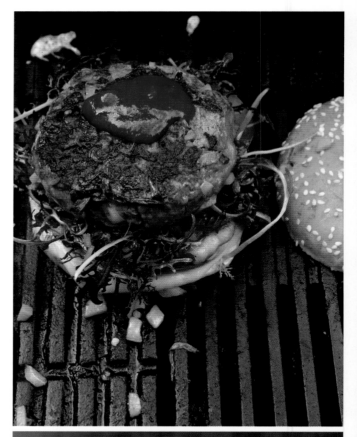

CLASSIC

For 6 hamburgers
Preparation time 10 minutes
Cooking time 5 minutes over high heat

1 sweet onion
6 hamburger patties (minced/ground beef)
6 slices bacon
6 hamburger buns
3 tablespoons tomato sauce (ketchup)
6 slices cheddar cheese
6 small lettuce leaves or a mixture
  of baby leaves

Slice the onion. Cook the hamburger patties, onion and the bacon over high heat. Toast the buns on the barbecue. Spread the buns with some tomato sauce and assemble the hamburgers, alternating all of the ingredients: cheddar, hamburger, bacon, onion, lettuce.

HAM

For 6 hamburgers
Preparation time 10 minutes
Cooking time 10 minutes over high heat

150 g (5½ oz) Comté cheese (or Gruyére)
3 bulb spring onions
3 thick slices of ham
6 thin slices of belly pork
6 hamburger buns
100 g (3½ oz) sundried tomatoes
1 bunch coriander (cilantro)
Sauce:
3 tablespoons mayonnaise
3 tablespoons tomato sauce (ketchup)
1 tablespoon cognac

Using a vegetable peeler, make slivers of Comté cheese.
Slice the bulb spring onions. Cut the slices of ham in two.
Cook the ham and the belly pork on the barbecue for
5 minutes. Lay the slices of Comté on top of the ham, leave
to melt in peace.
For the sauce, combine the mayonnaise with the tomato sauce
and cognac.
Toast the buns on the barbecue, spread with sauce and
assemble the burger with layers of ham, Comté, onions, pork,
sundried tomatoes, coriander.

CHICKEN

For 6 hamburgers
Preparation time 5 minutes
Cooking time 10 minutes over gentle heat on the hotplate

2 red onions
6 spears of green asparagus
6 hamburger buns
olive oil
6 chicken breast fillets
300 g (10½ oz) roquefort cheese
rocket (arugula)
salt and pepper

Peel and slice the onions, cut the aparagus spears in four and
cook the onions and asparagus on the hotplate until golden
brown. Drizzle the buns with some olive oil. Toast them on
the barbecue. Cook the chicken breasts for 7–8 minutes.
Cut the roquefort cheese into 6 slices, allow them to barely
melt on the hotplate. Dress the rocket with olive oil, salt and
pepper. Assemble the hamburger, making layers of asparagus,
chicken, roquefort, onions, rocket.

FOIE GRAS

For 6 hamburgers
Preparation time 10 minutes
Cooking time 10 minutes over gentle heat on the hotplate

2 duck breast fillets
50 g (1¾ oz) baby spinach leaves
6 hamburger buns
6 slices fresh foie gras
3 tablespoons wholegrain mustard
salt and pepper

Slash the skin of the duck breasts in a criss-cross pattern down
to the flesh. Cook the duck breasts over gentle heat 5 minutes
skin side, 2 minutes flesh side (they should stay red). Cut them
into thin slices.
Arrange the baby spinach leaves on a plate, cover them with
the duck breast. Toast the buns on the barbecue, cook the
slices of foie gras on the hotplate for about 1 minute on each
side. Spread the buns with mustard, assemble the hamburger
by piling on the duck, foie gras and spinach. Season.

EGG

For 6 hamburgers
Preparation time 15 minutes
Cooking time 10 minutes over high heat on the hotplate

1 sweet onion
1 cucumber
2 tomatoes
6 hamburger patties (minced/ground beef)
6 slices of speck (smoked ham or bacon)
6 hamburger buns
6 eggs
3 large spoonfuls Savora mustard
  (or American mustard)
3 tablespoons tomato sauce (ketchup)

Peel the onion, slice it with the cucumber and tomatoes.
Cook the hamburgers over high heat as well as the slices
of speck. Toast the buns on the barbecue grill, cook the eggs
on the hotplate. Spread the buns with mustard and tomato
sauce. Assemble the hamburgers, alternating all the ingredients:
hamburger, speck, egg, onion, cucumber, tomatoes.

Drink with: a quality beer, icy cold

HOT DOG

For 6 hot dogs
Preparation time 5 minutes
Cooking time 10 minutes over gentle heat on the hotplate

4 brown onions
2 tablespoons olive oil
1 teaspoon cumin
3 tablespoons tomato sauce (ketchup)
6 hot dog buns
6 lovely knack sausages (frankfurts or hot dogs)

Peel the onions, slice them thinly. Gently sauté them in olive oil on the hotplate until they're lightly brown, then add the cumin, tomato sauce and allow to caramelise.
Grill the sausages and bread on the barbecue grill. Spread the caramelised onions on the buns, place the sausages on top, cover with the other half of the bun. Watch out for falling onions!

TURKISH KEBAB

For 6 kebabs
Preparation time 15 minutes
Cooking time 15 minutes on the hotplate

600 g (1 lb 5 oz) lamb shoulder
6 Turkish bread rolls
2 sweet white onions
1 iceberg lettuce
salt and pepper
Sauce:
3 tablespoons créme fraiche or Greek yoghurt
1 tablespoon harissa

Cut the lamb shoulder into thin slices. Cook the lamb on the hotplate until it is well browned, season. Brown the rolls in the fat from the lamb. Peel the onions, shred the lettuce. For the sauce, combine the fromage blanc and harissa. Spread the buns with the fromage blanc-harissa sauce. Combine the lamb with the lettuce and onions. Top the buns with this mixture. Serve immediately.

BREAKFAST

For 6 breakfasts
Preparation time 10 minutes
Cooking time 10 minutes on the hotplate

3 sweet onions
6 slices of bacon
1 bunch coriander (cilantro)
6 eggs
6 English muffins
HP sauce (preferably classic woodsmoke flavour)

Peel and slice the onions, cook them on the hotplate with the bacon, add the leaves from the bunch coriander.
Cook the eggs on the hotplate. Toast the muffins, spread them with HP sauce, assemble the sandwich with layers of bacon, egg, coriander, onions.

CHORIZO OMELETTE

For 6 sandwichs
Preparation time 15 minutes
Cooking time 10 minutes on the hotplate

2 baguettes
1 garlic clove
olive oil
2 tomatoes
2 French shallots
12 eggs
salt and pepper
baby shiso leaves (purple mint/perilla)
12 slices chorizo sausage

Cut each baguette into three sections, split and rub them with garlic and drizzle with a little olive oil. Seed the tomatoes and dice the flesh. Peel and finely chop the French shallots.
Beat the eggs with a fork, add the French shallots and tomatoes, season. Cook 6 omelettes on the hotplate, add the shiso leaves.
Brown the slices of chorizo, then brown the bread in the fat from the chorizo. Place one omelette in each section of baguette and top it with two slices chorizo.

Drink with: beer again (there's some left over…)

VEGETARIAN BURGERS

With ultra-cooooool people

Serves 6
Preparation time 15 minutes
Cooking time 10 minutes on the hotplate

12 spears green asparagus
2 red onions
1 fennel bulb
3 green tomatoes
3 tablespoons crème fraîche
1 tablespoon tomato paste
6 soy burger patties
150 g (5½ oz/approx 1 cup) finely
  grated parmesan cheese
6 hamburger buns
1 handful rocket (arugula)
olive oil
salt and pepper

Cut the spears of asparagus in two lengthways, then into four
sections. Peel the onions, and slice them thinly along with the
fennel. Slice the green tomatoes into rounds.
Combine the crème fraîche with the tomato paste.
Cook the asparagus, red onions and fennel on the hotplate.
Make small mounds of parmesan cheese and brown to make
crisps. Cook the soy burgers. Brown the hamburger buns.
Dress the rocket with olive oil, season with salt and pepper.
Spread the buns with the crème fraîche-tomato paste mixture.
Assemble with layers of each ingredient: asparagus, soy burger,
parmesan, red onions, fennel, tomatoes, rocket.

Drink with: a greeeeen tea

CHAPTER IV

RIBS
&
CUT
LETS

THE LEGEND: BEEF RIB CUTLET

The beef rib cutlet (rib eye/côte de bœuf) or is synonymous with barbecue, the one is unimaginable without the other. Some have even wondered whether barbecue exists because of the beef rib cutlet, or if it's the other way around. They go together, but we will never know which came first. The beef rib cutlet is a stand-out dish which deserves special attention both when you choose the meat and when you cook it. The first stage is choosing your rib eye. It is wise to go to a butcher who will cut it in front of you—you can then choose the thickness according to the number of carnivores in your party; it should, as a minimum, weigh more than a kilo (2 lb 4 oz). The bone must be whole, never buy a rib whose bone has been cut in the middle, it won't have that extra bit of fat on the side, which provides that extra bit of gustatory pleasure so dear to our palate.

The beef needs to be aged to bring out its full taste and tenderness. Choose high quality beef to ensure good marbling, colour and flavour.

THE BEEF RIB CUTLET

With no one, I'm eating it all by myself, end of story!

Serves 1
Preparation time 5 minutes
Cooking time 20 minutes

1 beef rib cutlet (rib eye) weighing 1.2 kg (2 lb 10 oz)
sea salt

Light the coals, cook the beef 10 minutes each side, enjoy
at your leisure.

The cooking of the beef rib cutlet is of prime importance for
the perfect eating experience. It should be seared over high
heat to create a caramelised crust all over. This crust allows
you to imprison the juices inside the beef (allow 20 minutes
to cook a 1.2 kg (2 lb 6 oz) rib rare). It should rest for a few
minutes before being sacrificed to the raging hunger of that
day's guests. A beef rub cutlet on a barbecue makes the
ferocious appetite all the keener. Make sure you have
enough or risk a group sulk! Serve with the sea salt.

Drink with: none of your business

BLUE

WELL DONE

MEDIUM

RARE

FAR WEST RIBS

With a cowboy

Serves 6
Preparation time 10 minutes
Marinating time 12 hours
Cooking time 45 minutes in boiling water + 20 minutes
 over gentle heat

1.2 kg (2 lb 10 oz) pork spareribs
Marinade:
4 onions
6 garlic cloves
2 tablespoons herbes de Provençe (usually
 marjoram, oregano, rosemary, thyme)
1 tablespoon tomato paste
1 x 120 ml (approx 4 fl oz/½ cup) glass
 white wine
6 tablespoons tomato sauce (ketchup)
2 tablespoons HP sauce (preferably classic
 woodsmoke flavour)
2 tablespoons soy sauce
2 tablespoons Maggi seasoning sauce
1 tablespoon coarsely ground black pepper

Cook the spareribs for 45 minutes in gently simmering water.
For the marinade, peel the onions and garlic and finely chop
them. Combine all of the marinade ingredients. Reserve some
marinade for serving. Cover the spareribs with the remainder
of the marinade and chill for 12 hours.
Arrange the ribs over gentle heat, allow them to caramelise
at their leisure turning them regularly. Roll them in reserved
marinade before serving.

Drink with: brisk acidic rosé with intense fruitiness

PORK CHOP WITH HERBS

With a dietitian (pork is good, not fatty!)

Serves 6
Preparation time 15 minutes
Cooking time 20 minutes over gentle heat

6 pork chops
Herb salad:
1 bunch chervil
1 bunch coriander (cilantro)
½ bunch mint
2 lemons
3 bulb spring onions
3 tablespoons olive oil
salt and pepper

Cook the pork chops over gentle heat for 10 minutes each side: they should be well browned.
For the salad, pick the leaves from the bunches of herbs, keep them in the refrigerator. Juice and zest the lemons. Slice the bulb spring onions. Combine the herbs with the bulb spring onions, drizzle with olive oil, add the lemon zest and juice and season.
Serve the pork chops topped with the herb salad.

Drink with: sparkling mineral water (to please the dietitian)

PORK STEAKS & WHOLEGRAIN MUSTARD

With gusto

Serves 6
Preparation time 15 minutes
Cooking time 20 minutes over gentle heat

6 pork neck steaks (or pork scotch fillet)
Mustard crust:
2 egg whites
6 tablespoons wholegrain mustard
1 tablespoon herbes de Provençe (usually marjoram, oregano, rosemary, thyme)
salt and pepper

First make the mustard crust. Whisk the egg whites with a fork, add the wholegrain mustard and herbes de Provençe and season. Spread the chops with the egg white-mustard mixture, cook over gentle heat and on a clean barbecue grill for 20 minutes. Important: the less you turn your chops, the more the mustard crust will stay on the meat.

Drink with: good Gripa that lets you taste the soil and sun

EMMANUEL'S SPECIAL CUTLETS

With Emmanuel

Serves 6
Preparation time 10 minutes
Marinating time 3 hours
Cooking time 10 minutes over high heat

18 lamb cutlets
6 bulb spring onions
salt and pepper
Cider marinade:
8 garlic cloves
150 ml (5 fl oz/approx ⅔ cup) olive oil
200 ml (7 fl oz/approx ¾ cup) dry cider
1 tablespoon dried thyme
1 tablespoon dried rosemary

First make the marinade. Peel and crush the garlic. Gently brown the garlic in the olive oil. Combine with the cider, add the thyme and rosemary. Marinate the cutlets in the olive oil-cider mixture for 3 hours. Halve the bulb spring onions lengthways. Barbecue the cutlets with the onions over high heat, 1–2 minutes on each side (they should be well browned on the outside and juicy on the inside), season.

Drink with: dry cider

RACK OF LAMB WITH TAPENADE

With your partner's friends (that way you can stay beside the barbecue 'sorry not to be sitting down with you [yippee!], but I have to watch the food', without revealing the little interest you have in the dinner that's been imposed on you!)

Serves 6
Preparation time 15 minutes
Cooking time 20 minutes over gentle heat

3 racks of lamb
spicy salt (see page 18)
Tapenade:
200 g (7 oz) Kalamata olives
1 oxheart tomato
1 bunch rosemary
2 garlic cloves
6 anchovies in oil
150 ml (5 fl oz/approx ⅔ cup) olive oil
50 ml (approx 1¾ fl oz/3 tablespoons) cognac
1 bunch fresh thyme

Rub the racks of lamb with the spicy salt, cook them over gentle heat for about 20 minutes, making sure you turn them regularly. The fat dripping from the racks can catch alight, so you have to stay by the barbecue to watch over them. Separate the chops and top with tapenade.
For the tapenade, pit the olives. Cut the tomato into 1 cm (½ inch) thick slices. Place the tomato slices on the barbecue, burn the rosemary under the tomatoes, grill them 2 minutes each side. Dice the grilled tomatoes. Roughly process the olives with the garlic, anchovies, cognac and olive oil, add the diced tomato and the leaves picked from the bunch of thyme.

Drink with: truly great red—magnum bottle (you need some compensation, after all!)

VEAL CHOPS WITH SHALLOT BUTTER

With your GOOD blood test results. That's right, I have no cholesterol!

Serves 6
Preparation time 15 minutes
Cooking time 10 to 15 minutes over high heat

3 thick veal chops
Shallot butter:
1 garlic clove
2 French shallots
1 bunch chives
150 g (5½ oz) demi-sel (lightly salted) butter
1 teaspoon coarsely ground black pepper

For the butter, peel and finely chop the garlic and French shallots. Snip the chives into small sections. Using a fork, work the butter until it is soft and incorporate the garlic, pepper, French shallots and chives. Keep the butter at room temperature.
Cook the veal chops over high heat for 10–15 minutes (according to thickness and how you like it cooked).
Spread generously with the shallot butter, serve immediately.

Drink with: Burgundian-style red with a torrent of fruit (magnum bottle). That's right, no triglycerides either!

152

CHAPTER V

BAR
BE
CUE
XXL

WHOLE ROASTS

Whole roasts are to the barbecue what three Michelin stars are to gastronomy: a must.

In summer, there's always something to celebrate. The barbecue will then show its XXL face. No more individual skewers, you throw yourself into large-scale catering, you plan big.

If you're talking whole roasts, you're talking slow cooking, and everything this implies in terms of preparation. The night before, you dig a hole to make a home for your half-barrel, you put your load of wood inside, an old newspaper and a box of matches.

You make a marinade: olive oil, white wine, herbs, mustard which will refresh the beast throughout the long cooking and give it the desired flavours.

On the day, you get up early (5 or 6 in the morning, prior to the commencement of hostilities) to prepare the embers. The cooking needs to be gentle to obtain a crisp skin and well-cooked, juicy meat inside. Cooking time depends on the size of the piece being cooked, patience is the order of the day. You need arms willing and able to turn a spit: allow a quantity of chilled rosé to motivate the troops. This even regular cooking is the key to the success of your roasted lamb, pig or any other animal.

The cooking is finished, the knives are sharpened, jaws are clenched ready for battle. The carving starts, plates jostle, congratulations ring out on all sides, it certainly deserves 'three stars'!

x1

x1

x1 x2 x38

x2

x5

'TOADED' CHICKEN WITH MUSTARD

With a prince charming

Serves 6
Preparation time 20 minutes
Marinating time 24 hours
Cooking time 45 minutes over gentle heat

1 beautiful free-range chicken
salt and pepper
1 bunch flat-leafed parsley
1 bunch spring onions (scallions)
Marinade:
6 garlic cloves
4 tablespoons dijon mustard
1 tablespoon honey
1 teaspoon dried oregano
2 tablespoons olive oil

Cut open the breast side of the chicken and flatten it out
by pressing down hard (it will then look like a large toad).
For the marinade, peel and chop the garlic. Combine all
of the marinade ingredients: garlic, mustard, honey, oregano,
olive oil.
Lay the chicken down in a dish, spread over this marinade
(on both sides), season, cover with plastic wrap, chill for
24 hours.
Place the chicken over gentle heat, and cook it for 45 minutes,
turning from time to time. Once the chicken is cooked,
scatter with chopped parsley and spring onions and cover
for 2 minutes so they soften. Serve immediately.

Drink with: any princely wine

CAJUN-STYLE CHICKEN

With a banjo player

Serves 6
Preparation time 20 minutes
Marinating time 24 hours
Cooking time 1 hour over gentle heat, covered

1 beautiful free-range chicken
1 small soft cheese (such as Boursin or cream
  cheese flavoured with herbs and garlic)
Marinade:
8 garlic cloves
2 tablespoons ground piment d'Espelette
  (or hot paprika)
2 tablespoons herbes de Provençe (usually
  marjoram, oregano, rosemary, thyme)
2 tablespoons paprika
4 tablespoons olive oil
juice of one lemon
salt and pepper

For the marinade, peel and slice the garlic. Combine with the
piment d'Espelette, herbes de Provençe, paprika, olive oil and
lemon juice, season.
Combine the Boursin cheese with 2 spoonfuls of this marinade
and place inside the chicken. Massage the chicken with the rest
of the marinade, rubbing it in well. Keep in the refrigerator for
24 hours.
Cook the chicken over gentle heat, covered, for 1 hour, turning
it from time to time. Cut up the chicken and dress it with the
cheese that has melted during cooking.

Drink with: fresh light red with a distinct violet aroma

SPIT-ROASTED SUCKLING PIG

**With the whole family as long as its a large one.
Set the alarm for 5 am to prepare the embers.**

Serves 20+
Preparation time 30 minutes
Cooking time 3 hours over gentle heat

1 suckling pig, weighing 20 kg (approx 40 lb)
Marinade:
30 garlic cloves
10 onions
6 dried chillis
6 bay leaves
500 g (1 lb 2 oz) dijon mustard
1 litre (35 fl oz/4 cups) olive oil
1 bottle white wine
Stuffing:
6 onions
8 carrots
8 granny smith apples
250 g (9 oz) brioche
1 litre (35 fl oz/4 cups) crème fraîche
2 kg (4 lb 8 oz) sausagemeat
1 tablespoon juniper berries
2 branches rosemary
2 sprigs fresh thyme
2 bay leaves
150 ml (5 fl oz/approx ⅔ cup) cognac
salt and pepper

To make the marinade, peel the garlic and onions. Chop them
up finely with the chillies and bay leaves, combine with the
mustard, olive oil and white wine.
For the stuffing, peel the onions, carrots and apples. Slice the
onions and cut the carrots and apples into segments. Cut the
brioche into cubes and soak in the crème fraîche. Combine
all the stuffing ingredients together, mixing well, and season.
Stuff the pig with this mixture, sew up the belly with metal
thread. Place the pig on the spit, wrap the ears in foil. Tie
together the back legs and front legs.
Place the pig over gentle heat for 3 hours, basting regularly
with marinade (make sure you have some wood coal handy in
case the embers from the morning are not enough). It needs to
cook slowly and gently so the skin can caramelise at its leisure
while the meat cooks in peace. Ask your favourite uncle to
lend you a hand carving the pig.

**Drink with: the little red that your uncle Jack brought
back in the 20-litre cask from his trip to the vineyards**

SPIT-ROASTED LAMB

With all your friends…the ones who could be bothered with the trip…Same wake-up time as for the pig, there's no helping it!

Serves 20
Preparation time 45 minutes
Cooking time 3 hours over gentle heat

1 lamb, weighing 15 kg (33 lb)
Rocket Marinade:
200 g (7 oz) rocket (arugula)
500 ml (17 fl oz/2 cups) olive oil
500 ml (17 fl oz/2 cups) white port
juice of 2 lemons
6 garlic cloves, peeled
salt and pepper
Pesto:
6 bunches basil
1 litre (35 fl oz/4 cups) olive oil
200 g (7 oz) parmesan cheese
3 French shallots, peeled
100 g (3½ oz/⅔ cup) pine nuts
2 garlic cloves, peeled
salt and pepper
Chilli Marinade:
5 bird's eye chillis
1 tablespoon tomato paste
6 tablespoons brown sugar
juice of 3 lemons
6 garlic cloves, peeled
500 ml (17 fl oz/2 cups) sunflower oil
200 ml (7 fl oz/approx ¾ cup) rice vinegar
200 ml (7 fl oz/approx ¾ cup) pineapple juice
salt and pepper
Tomato Marinade:
400 g (14 oz) sundried tomatoes in oil
4 tablespoons tomato sauce (ketchup)
1 tablespoon dried thyme
1 small can anchovies in oil
750 ml (26 fl oz/3 cups) olive oil
salt and pepper

Lamb meat is tender and delicate. Spit roasted lamb, using woodfire cooking, will take the flavour to a new level. Put the lamb on the spit with its front and hind legs attached to the spit. Cook for a leisurely 3 hours, regularly massaging it with your choice of marinade.
To make the marinades and pesto, process all the ingredients for each together and let the guests choose. Reserve some of each for serving and use the rest for basting.

Drink with: the little rosé that Nick brought back in a 10-litre cask (he's not as strong as uncle Jack!!) from his neck of the woods

CHAPTER VI

HIGH & LOW TIDE

REELY GOOD...

Saturday arrives with a sun capable of tanning hides in under 2 minutes and your sandals (size 11 if you please), wait impatiently beside the door. You're going camping. Summer was crying out to 'hit the road', the boot is overflowing with baggage, the roofrack is fully booked. You're packed like sardines in the car, a fishing rod between your toes, but it doesn't matter, you're happy. Happy to be facing 12 hours in the car, happy to imagine the future barbecues at nightfall.

It's been a week now since the tent was put up, a week since the rod was set up, a week with nothing on the barbecue but sausages...It is high time you realised that the fish shop is the best fishing spot. Red mullet, bass, john dory, mackerels and sardines are all there thumbing their noses at us, a reminder of the hours spent on the rocks dreaming of such miracles. It's game on for a fish grill.

You use good hot coals to caramelise the skin while keeping the inside juicy. The cooking needs to be quick and well controlled, the barbecue gets its summer sheen back, it's time for champagne!

BASS WITH FENNEL

With fishing friends (to show off!)

Serves 6
Preparation time 20 minutes
Cooking time 30 minutes over high heat

2 sea bass, each weighing
1.2 kg (2 lb 10 oz)
2 tablespoons fennel seeds
few stalks of wild fennel or
  1 bunch dill
sea salt
Marinade:
3 tomatoes
1 spring onion (scallion)
1 bunch chives
1 punnet redcurrants
2 tablespoons light soy sauce
200 ml (7 fl oz/approx ¾ cup) olive oil

Clean and gut the bass, remove the gills, fill the cavity with the fennel seeds and wild fennel.
For the marinade, plunge the tomatoes in boiling water for 10 seconds, remove the skin. Dice the flesh. Finely chop the spring onion, chop the chives, pick the redcurrants off the bunch. Combine all the marinade ingredients with the soy sauce and olive oil.
Cook the bass for 15 minutes on each side (wait for the the first side to be well browned before turning the fish, or the skin will stick to the grill). Remove the fish, drizzle with marinade, season with sea salt.

Drink with: organic chablis at slightly colder than cellar temperature

BLACK SEABREAM

With our new friends

Serves 6
Preparation time 15 minutes
Cooking time 20 minutes over high heat

3 black seabream, each weighing 400 g (14 oz)
sea salt
200 ml (7 fl oz/approx ¾ cup) olive oil
Stuffing:
80 g (2¾ oz) Kalamata olives
4 bulb spring onions
3 beautiful very ripe tomatoes
2 sprigs lemon thyme

Brush the cleaned bream with some of the olive oil.
For the stuffing, pit the olives, and roughly chop them.
Finely slice the bulb spring onions, finely dice the tomatoes,
pick the leaves from the thyme, combine everything.
Stuff the bream with a third of this mixture. Season the fish
with sea salt. Combine the rest of the stuffing mixture with
the remainder of the olive oil to make a marinade and set
aside. Barbecue the bream over high heat, 10 minutes each
side (the point of a knife should easily reach the backbone).
Remove the fillets and coat with marinade.

Drink with: crisp clean sauvignon blanc

JOHN DORY

With your religious friends

Serves 6
Preparation time 15 minutes
Cooking time 20 minutes over high heat

3 beautiful john dory
Shallot-tomato compote:
2 fresh tomatoes
2 French shallots
1 glass dry white wine (approx 125 ml/4 fl oz/½ cup)
1 tablespoon brown sugar
100 g (3½ oz) sundried tomatoes in oil
salt and pepper
1 bunch fresh thyme

Cut the head off each fish, Amen.
For the compote, plunge the fresh tomatoes into boiling water
for 30 seconds and peel them. Seed the tomatoes and keep the
flesh. Peel and slice the French shallots, cook them over a low
heat in a saucepan in the white wine with the sugar. Add the
sundried tomatoes and the fresh tomatoes and cook until you
have a thick compote. Season, add the leaves of the fresh thyme.
Cook the fish over high heat for 10 minutes each side. Remove
and serve with the compote.

Drink with: communion wine

MACKEREL
WITH LEMON

With people you don't want to be seen with

Serves 6
Preparation time 20 minutes
Cooking time 10 minutes over high heat

6 mackerels
sea salt
Lemon marinade:
3 eggs
3 lemons
50 g (1¾ oz) caperberries
200 ml (7 fl oz/approx ¾ cup) olive oil

Clean the mackerel.
For the marinade, boil the eggs for 10 minutes, run them
under cold water, peel and roughly chop them. Zest two of the
lemons, take out the segments of all three lemons, removing all
skin and pith. Slice the caperberries, combine all the ingredients
with the olive oil.
Cook the mackerel 5 minutes each side. Remove the fish
and drizzle with the marinade and season with sea salt.

**Drink with: light green gold sauvignon blanc with a nose
of celery, unripe apples and blackboard chalk**

SARDINES

With the neighbours—avoiding the problem of the smell

Serves 6
Preparation time 15 minutes
Cooking time 5 minutes over high heat

24 very fresh sardines
2 baguettes
sea salt
Herb-garlic olive oil:
6 garlic cloves
150 ml (5 fl oz/approx ⅔ cup) olive oil
1 tablespoon herbes de Provençe (usually
  marjoram, oregano, rosemary, thyme)

Purists do not gut sardines, the rest do.
For the herb-garlic mixture, peel the garlic, and slice it thinly.
Gently heat the olive oil, add the garlic until it takes on a
golden brown color, then add the herbes de Provençe.
Grill slices of baguette on the barbecue. Cook the sardines
over high heat 2–3 minutes each side and take out the fillets
(with your fingers).
Dip the grilled bread in the garlic olive oil, arrange the sardine
fillets on top and sprinkle with sea salt.

Drink with: whatever the neighbours brought

RED MULLET
LIVER TOASTS

With a passionate fisherman

Serves 6
Preparation time 20 minutes
Cooking time 10 minutes over high heat and on the hotplate

6 beautiful red mullets
6 slices baguette
3 sprigs dried thyme
12 pickling onions
12 Kalamata olives
1 bunch flat-leafed parsley
100 ml (3½ fl oz/approx ½ cup) olive oil
salt and pepper

Clean the red mullet, taking care to reserve the liver, rinse
the fish and add the dried thyme. Peel and slice the pickling
onions, pit and slice the olives, pick the leaves from the parsley.
Sauté these ingredients with the liver on the hotplate in a
little olive oil, season.
Drizzle the slices of baguette with olive oil, grill them on
the barbecue. Top them with the liver-onion-olive mixture.
Barbecue the mullet over high heat 5 minutes each side.
Serve with the toast.

**Drink with: red wine for the red mullet—a nutty wine
showing crushed almonds, hazelnuts and macadamia on
top of cranberry and figs.**

ANCHOVIES ON TOAST

With whoever drops in for drinks

Serves 6
Preparation time 10 minutes
Cooking time 5 minutes over high heat and on the hotplate

1 baguette
2 garlic cloves
200 ml (7 fl oz/approx ¾ cup) olive oil
6 bulb spring onions
3 ripe tomatoes
12 fresh anchovies
sea salt and pepper

Slice the baguette lengthways to make large toasts. Peel the
garlic, rub over the bread. Drizzle each slice with some olive oil.
Slice the bulb spring onions, cut the tomatoes into segments.
Sauté the tomatoes and onions on the hotplate in a little
olive oil.
Barbecue the whole anchovies 2 minutes over high heat, remove
the fillets with your fingers and grill the slices of baguette on the
barbecue.
Top each slice with the tomato-onion mixture, arrange
the anchovy fillets on top, season with sea salt and pepper.

Drink with: smooth and fruity white with stony citrus nose

CUTTLEFISH

With Loïc Perron or any other famous sailor you know

Serves 6
Preparation time 15 minutes
Cooking time 5 minutes over high heat

6 cleaned cuttlefish
salt and pepper
Marinade:
2 lemongrass stems
2 spring onions (scallions)
1 bunch dill
150 ml (5 fl oz/approx ⅔ cup) olive oil
1 teaspoon brown sugar
juice of 1 lemon
1 teaspoon curry powder
1 tablespoon fish sauce

Using a utility knife or box cutter (with the blade extended to half the thickness of the cuttlefish), slash the outside (rounded side) of the cuttlefish in a criss-cross pattern.
For the marinade, finely slice the lemongrass and spring onions, pick the leaves from the dill. Combine these ingredients with the olive oil, sugar, lemon juice, curry powder and fish sauce.
Barbecue the cuttlefish, slashed side down, for 3 minutes, then 2 minutes on the other side. Warning: cuttlefish cooks quickly and becomes tough when overcooked. Drizzle the cuttlefish with the marinade, season.

Drink with: summer quaffing white revealing honeysuckle and plenty of fruit

SHALLOT–LIME YELLOWFIN TUNA

With a meat-lover (yes, that's right!)

Serves 6
Preparation time 15 minutes
Marinating time 24 hours
Cooking time 15 minutes over high heat

6 echalions (banana shallots or elongated
  French shallots)
6 fillets yellowfin tuna
sea salt
Marinade:
2 limes
200 ml (7 fl oz/approx ¾ cup) olive oil
1 teaspoon ground cardamom

For the marinade, zest and juice the limes and combine with the olive oil and cardamom. Reserve a little for serving.
Marinate the tuna in the marinade for 24 hours.
Peel the echalions, cut them in half. Cook the echalions on the barbecue for 15 minutes. Drizzle the echalions with the reserved marinade, season with sea salt. Serve immediately with tuna.
Sear the tuna fillets according to how each person likes it cooked.

Drink with: varietal Viognier

SALMON SAUCE VERTE

With friends of your dieting husband

Serves 6
Preparation time 20 minutes
Cooking time 15 minutes over high heat

1 salmon fillet
Sauce verte:
2 eggs
1 tablespoon strong mustard
1 bunch basil, leaves pulled
1 tablespoon rice vinegar
juice of 1 lemon
200 ml (7 fl oz/approx ¾ cup) olive oil
salt and pepper

Remove the salmon bones using tweezers.
For the sauce verte, bring a saucepan of water to the boil, immerse the eggs for 5 minutes, refresh them under cold water and peel them. Process the eggs with the mustard, basil leaves, rice vinegar, lemon juice and olive oil, season.
Place the salmon skin-side down on a very hot barbecue grill, cook for 5 minutes, turn the salmon over and cook a further 5 minutes. Remove the skin and place it flesh-side down on the barbecue for 5 minutes. Serve the salmon fillet while the skin is still crispy. Serve the sauce verte separately.

Drink with: clean pumped up chardonnay

KING PRAWNS WITH FENNEL

With someone you love, they're expensive!

Serves 6
Preparation time 10 minutes
Cooking time 5 minutes over high heat, covered

18 beautiful king prawns (jumbo shrimp)
2 tablespoons pastis (aniseed flavoured liqueur)
1 bunch wild fennel
1 tablespoon fennel seeds
sea salt

Drizzle the prawns with pastis, cook them on the barbecue for 3 minutes, covered. Place the fennel on top of the prawns and cover again for 2 minutes.
Serve immediately, sprinkle with fennel seeds and season with sea salt.

Drink with: champagne, while you're at it

TARRAGON SQUID

With a Jules Verne enthusiast

Serves 6
Preparation time 20 minutes
Cooking time 10 minutes over high heat

6 beautiful squid, each weighing 200 g (7 oz)
1 teaspoon ground paprika
olive oil
Stuffing:
1 bunch tarragon
2 French shallots
150 g (5½ oz) shelled pistachios
2 slices soft white sandwich bread
150 ml (5 fl oz/approx ⅔ cup) cream
2 eggs
200 g (7 oz/approx 1¼ cups) cooked rice
salt and pepper

Clean the squid, making sure you reserve the tentacles, and rinse them thoroughly.
For the stuffing, pick the leaves from the tarragon, finely chop the French shallots. Process together the tarragon, pistachios, bread, cream and eggs. Add the French shallots and rice, season. Stuff the squid with this mixture, reposition the tentacles and attach them to the base with a toothpick. Sprinkle with paprika. Cook 5 minutes over high heat on each side. Drizzle with some olive oil.

Drink with: white burgundy loaded with an assault of orange peel and honey

EXECUTED LOBSTER

With an executioner

Serves 6
Freezer time: 1 hour
Preparation time 15 minutes
Cooking time 10 minutes over high heat

6 live lobsters
Herb butter:
1 French shallot
2 garlic cloves
1 tablespoon olive oil
1 bunch tarragon
½ bunch curly-leaf parsley
100 g (3½ oz) demi-sel (lightly salted) butter
salt and pepper

Place the lobsters in the freezer for about 1 hour to render them unconscious.
For the herb butter, peel and finely chop the French shallot. Peel and chop the garlic. Soften the shallot and garlic gently in the olive oil. Pick the leaves from the tarragon and parsley, process them with the butter and softened garlic and shallot, season and keep at room temperature.
Remove the lobsters from the freezer. Hold the lobster with the head facing you, shell-side down. Using a sharp chef's knife, cut the lobster in two by inserting the knife where the head meets the tail. Split the head, then the tail.
Sear the lobsters on the barbecue grill, 7–8 minutes shell-side down, and 2 minutes flesh side down. Spread the flesh with the herb butter.

Drink with: chardonnay that steps up in intensity as you taste

KING PRAWNS AND SPRING VEGETABLES

With friends who didn't want to come – 'it's spring, we're watching what we eat'. I have just what you need.

Serves 6
Preparation time 20 minutes
Cooking time 5 minutes over high heat on the hotplate

18 beautiful king prawns (jumbo shrimp)
150 g (5½ oz) snow peas (mangetouts)
150 g (5½ oz) green beans
12 spears of green asparagus
6 baby carrots
150 g (5½ oz) podded broad beans
15 g (½ oz/1 tablespoon) butter
salt and pepper
Marinade:
2 garlic cloves
juice of one lemon
3 tablespoons soy sauce
1 tablespoon pastis (aniseed flavoured liqueur)

Peel and devein the prawns.
For the marinade, peel and crush the garlic, mix with the lemon juice, soy sauce and pastis. Drizzle the prawns with this marinade. Reserve a little for deglazing.
Poach all the vegetables in boiling water and refresh them immediately. Melt the butter on the hotplate, add all of the vegetables, cook them 5 minutes and deglaze with the reserved prawn marinade.
Barbecue the prawns 2 minutes each side. Serve immediately with the vegetables.

Drink with: sparkling mineral water, to annoy the people who initially didn't want to come

SCALLOPS WITH GRILLED LETTUCE

With a lover or lovers

Serves 6
Preparation time 10 minutes
Cooking time 5 minutes over high heat

3 baby cos lettuces (small romaine)
1 tablespoon olive oil
12 scallops
6 thin slices speck (smoked ham or bacon)
Shallot vinaigrette:
3 French shallots
150 ml (5 fl oz/approx ⅔ cup) olive oil
1 tablespoon balsamic vinegar
1 teaspoon Savora mustard (or American mustard)

Remove the scallops from their shell and remove their roe.
For the vinaigrette, peel and finely slice the French shallots.
Combine the shallots with the olive oil, balsamic vinegar and Savora mustard.
Halve the lettuces lengthways, brush them with olive oil.
Barbecue the scallops 2 minutes each side (they should be almost raw in the middle). Barbecue the speck until it is crispy, sear the sucrine lettuces on the grill.
Arrange the scallops on a plate, add the lettuce, the speck, roughly sliced, and drizzle with the shallot vinaigrette.

Drink with: crisp, dry and invigorating muscadet or your favourite seafood wine

SCALLOPS AND SPECK

With pilgrims on the way to Bali

Serves 6
Preparation time 20 minutes
Cooking time 10 minutes on the hotplate

18 scallops
4 carrots
1 French shallot
2 garlic cloves
1 orange beetroot
6 slices speck (smoked ham or bacon)
1 bunch chives
2 tablespoons canola oil
salt and pepper

Remove the scallops from their shell and remove their roe.
Peel the carrots, cut them into 3 x 5 mm (⅛ x ¼ inch) sticks (julienne). Peel and finely chop the French shallot and the garlic. Peel the beetroot and cut it into thin julienne strips.
Snip the chives into 2 cm (¾ inch) lengths. Slice the speck into strips.
Sauté the vegetables and the speck on the hotplate with the canola oil for 5 minutes. Sear the scallops 2–3 minutes each side. Add the chives to the vegetables, season.
Serve immediately.

Drink with: refined and delicate riesling

ROAST SALMON

With a seachanger

Serves 6
Preparation time 15 minutes
Cooking time 15 minutes over high heat

1 beautiful salmon fillet weighing about
  1.2 kg (2 lb 10 oz), skin on
1 tablespoon fennel seeds
salt and pepper
oil
Seasoning:
2 French shallots
1 bunch coriander (cilantro)
1 lemon
1 small bird's eye chilli

Cut off the thin end of the salmon. Remove the bones using
a pair of tweezers. Make an incision along the length of the
salmon where the belly meets the loin, sliding the knife
between the belly meat and the skin. Remove the belly meat
(you could eat it tartare as an appetiser). You will then have
a core of salmon meat with extra skin on the side.
For the seasoning, peel and finely chop the French shallots.
Pick the leaves from the coriander and roughly chop them.
Zest the lemon. Chop up the bird's eye chilli, removing
the seeds.
Season the salmon loin with the seasoning and fennel seeds,
season with salt and pepper. Roll the loin in its skin and tie
it up with cooking twine soaked in salted water. Cook for
15 minutes in a little oil over high heat, turning the salmon
at regular intervals. Serve in generous slices with the crispy
skin.

Drink with: chardonnay, pure and simple

ROAST MONKFISH

With a keen hunter who's turning to fish

Serves 6
Preparation time 30 minutes
Cooking time 20 minutes over gentle heat, covered

2 monkfish tails, each weighing 800 g (1 lb 12 oz)
 or any firm fleshed fish
18 thin slices of speck (smoked ham or bacon)
Sundried tomato purée:
1 bunch basil
1 garlic clove
20 g (¾ oz) fresh ginger
1 orange
100 g (3½ oz) sundried tomatoes in oil
salt and pepper

Separate the monkfish fillets from the central backbone.
Remove the thin membrane that covers the fillets.
For the purée, pick the leaves from the basil, peel the garlic and
ginger, juice and zest the orange. Process together the sun-dried
tomatoes, basil, orange zest, ginger and garlic. Loosen the purée
with the orange juice (it should have a smooth and creamy
texture), season.
Lay out the slices of speck, overlapping them slightly: the row
needs to be the same length as the monkfish. Lay a monkfish
fillet down with the thicker end towards you. Spread with
tomato purée, cover with another monkfish fillet (thick end
pointing the other way), roll in the speck.
Cook the monkfish over gentle heat (place the side where
the slices of speck 'join' down first). Cover, allow to cook for
10 minutes, then turn the roast over for a further 10 minutes.

Drink with: burgundy (or white for the purists)

SALMON ON FIR

With the vegetarians of the high plains

Serves 6
Preparation time 20 minutes
Cooking time 5 minutes over high heat, covered

1 salmon fillet
6 fir tree branches
salt and pepper
Marinade:
200 ml (7 fl oz/approx ¾ cup) olive oil
juice of 2 lemons
1 tablespoon miel de sapin (fir tree honey)

Remove the skin from the salmon fillet, remove the bones using
a pair of tweezers. Make thin slices of salmon, cutting from the
thicker end towards the tail.
For the marinade, combine the olive oil with the lemon juice,
add the honey.
Wrap the fir branches in slices of salmon, swaddling the
branches where the needles are and brush with marinade.
Place the fir on the barbecue, cover and cook for 5 minutes.
The salmon should stay pink in the centre.
Serve the salmon on the fir branches and season.

Drink with: chenin blanc leaving the palate clean and dry

FINGER BURNERS

You weren't very good at line fishing, but we'll make up for it with some fishing by hand. Today we're preparing for a veritable shellfish hunt.

Knives, gloves, flippers, yabby pump nothing is left to chance. We need to forget the humiliation of the first week, when the by-word was 'empty-handed'! You spot a few well-watered rocks by the sea, to which mussels are clinging en masse. You divide the labour: one in the water to pick them from the bunch, one on the rock to collect and clean the booty, and you start to get back a little credibility. Small holes with air bubbles in the wet sand suggest the hidden presence of cockles or pippies. He is a mistrustful creature, but with a quick shuffle with your toes, wham, you seize the beast, pluck him from his home, and wear a winner's grin.

When you're a Robinson Crusoe like an urban *Survivor*— guitar under the arm, bag of shellfish and dirty hair—you must be in for a special night of cooking. You light the fire, place that day's treasure on the flames and sing sea shanties in a true communion with Mother Nature.

SHELL
FISH
HUNT

RAZOR CLAMS WITH TARRAGON BUTTER

With a family that goes barefoot

Serves 6
Preparation time 10 minutes
Cooking time 5 minutes over high heat

36 fresh razor clams
Tarragon butter:
1 bunch tarragon
2 French shallots
150 g (5½ oz) demi-sel (lightly salted) butter

For the tarrogan butter, pick the leaves from the tarragon.
Peel and finely slice the French shallots, process the shallots
and tarragon with the butter.
Arrange the razor clams over the hot coals, flesh side down,
for 5 minutes until they take on a golden colour.
Melt the tarragon butter in a saucepan and drizzle over the
razor clams. Swallow the razors, walk on the coals.

Drink with: an aromatic white (preferably from the Rhône)

THE GROUND-DWELLERS

Still with the same crowd

Serves 6
Preparation time 15 minutes
Cooking time 5 minutes

mussels
oysters
razor clams
hard-shell clams
other kinds of clam
and everything in the way of shellfish that
 the day's fishing trip has brought in

Make a cosy bed out of pine needles (like a country mattress that moulds to your body, thick like a brioche fresh out of the oven). On this mattress arrange all kinds of shellfish, and light the fire like the Johnny Hallyday song: "*allumer le feu, allumer le feu, et faire danser les diables et les dieux, allumer le feu, allumer le feu, et voir grandir la flamme dans vos yeux, allumer le feu...*"
Enjoy sitting on the ground, bring the guitar out and "*allumer le feu, allumer le feu, et faire danser les diables et les dieux...*".

Drink with: whatever's left at the bottom of the icebox, if indeed there is anything left

ÉCLADE

With passing friends

Serves 6
Preparation time 15 minutes
Cooking time 5 minutes

3 kg (6 lb 12 oz) mussels
dozens of pine needles that the
    children have gathered

Arrange the mussels in a large pan (like a paella pan), with
the pointed (hinge) end upwards—when the mussel opens,
it mustn't fill with ash. Cover generously with very dry pine
needles, shoo the children back to a safe distance, light the
needles, wait for the mussels to open.
Enjoy from the pan.

Drink with: the fruity white in the back of the fridge

CHAPTER VII

THE
BITS
ON THE
SIDE

POTATOES
IN EMBERS

Serves 6
Preparation time 15 minutes
Cooking time 30 minutes in slow coals

6 beautiful potatoes

Wrap the potatoes in foil. Place them right on the embers,
cover with more embers for about 30 minutes. The potato
needs to be soft to the touch.
Serve with the accompaniments below.

TARRAGON CREAM

1 bunch tarragon
1 French shallot
4 tablespoons Greek yoghurt
2 tablespoons crème fraîche
salt and pepper

Pick the leaves from the bunch of tarragon and chop them
finely. Peel and finely chop the French shallot. Combine
everything with the yoghurt and crème fraîche, season.

PISTACHIO PESTO

1 bunch basil
150 g (5½ oz) pistachios
200 ml (7 fl oz/approx ¾ cup) olive oil
50 g (1¾ oz) parmesan cheese
1 French shallot
salt and pepper

Pick the leaves from the basil. Process the pistachios, basil,
olive oil and parmesan cheese, season. Peel and finely chop
the French shallot, add it to the pistachio pesto.

SAUCE VIERGE

3 ripe tomatoes
1 bunch basil
2 bulb spring onions
1 tablespoon capers
200 ml (7 fl oz/approx ¾ cup) olive oil
salt and pepper

Plunge the tomatoes into boiling water for 30 seconds,
remove the skin and finely dice the flesh. Pick the leaves
from the basil and finely chop them, chop the bulb
spring onions. Combine everything with the capers
and olive oil, season.

SPICED TOMATOES

6 tomatoes
2 garlic cloves
1 onion
30 g (1 oz) ginger
3 tablespoons olive oil
1 tablespoon soy sauce
salt and pepper

Plunge the tomatoes into boiling water for 30 seconds, remove
the skin and finely dice the flesh. Peel and chop the garlic,
onion and ginger. Gently sauté this mixture in the olive oil,
add the diced tomato and allow to stew together.
Process everything together, add the soy sauce, season.

ONIONS WITH PEPPER BUTTER

Serves 6
Preparation time 5 minutes
Cooking time 15 minutes over gentle heat

6 beautiful brown onions
120 g (4¼ oz) demi-sel (lightly salted) butter
1 teaspoon sichuan peppercorns
1 teaspoon coarsely ground black pepper

Cut a cross in the top of the onions, cutting two thirds of
the way down. Place 20 g (¾ oz) butter inside each onion,
season with a combination of peppers.
Wrap the onions in foil, place them directly on the embers,
cover them with more embers (cross facing upwards)
for 15 minutes. The onions should be soft to the touch.
Serve with barbecued fish or offal—the acidic note of
the onions goes well with them.

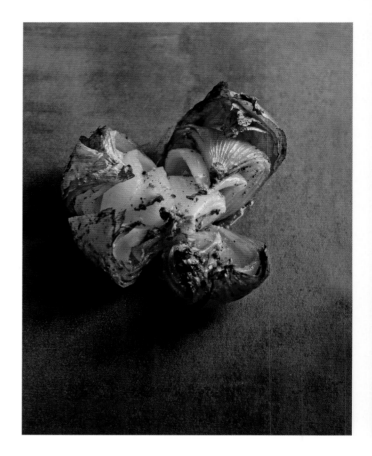

YOUNG GARLIC

Serves 6
Preparation time 5 minutes
Cooking time 15 minutes over gentle heat

3 heads of garlic
60 g (2¼ oz) demi-sel (lightly salted) butter
1 tablespoon herbes de Provençe (usually
   marjoram, oregano, rosemary, thyme)
1 sprig fresh thyme

Slice the top off the heads of garlic. Place a pat of butter on
each head, scatter with herbes de Provençe and fresh thyme
leaves. Place the top back on the garlic.
Wrap each head of garlic in foil. Place over gentle heat for
15 minutes. Serve alongside barbecued meat.

TOMATOES WITH LEMON THYME

Serves 6
Preparation time 10 minutes
Cooking time 5 minutes over high heat

12 black krim tomatoes
6 French shallots
100 ml (3½ fl oz/approx ½ cup) olive oil
1 bunch lemon thyme
sea salt

Remove the tomato stems and cut the tomatoes in half. Peel the French shallots and cut them in half. On a barbecue grill that's been oiled and is nice and hot, arrange the tomatoes and shallots, cover with lemon thyme. Cover with a cloche (see note) and cook for 5 minutes. Serve drizzled with some olive oil, season with seal salt.

Note: You can make a cloche from foil.

CAPSICUM + CHORIZO

Serves 6
Preparation time 30 minutes
Cooking time 15 minutes over high heat and on the hotplate

2 red capsicums (peppers)
2 green capsicums (peppers)
2 yellow capsicums (peppers)
6 garlic cloves
150 g (5½ oz) spicy chorizo sausage
150 ml (5 fl oz/approx ⅔ cup) olive oil
salt and pepper

Barbecue the capsicums whole over high heat, until their skin blackens and puffs up. Seal them inside a plastic bag for 20 minutes. Remove the skin and cut the capsicums into strips. Peel and finely slice the garlic cloves. Julienne the chorizo sausage. Sauté the chorizo and garlic on the hotplate in the olive oil, top the capsicums with this mixture, add a drizzle of olive oil, season.
This mixture keeps for one week, covered with olive oil.
These capsicums are the perfect accompaniment to barbecued meats such as a lamb dish.

CORN

Serves 6
Preparation time 5 minutes
Cooking time 5 minutes in simmering water + 5 minutes over gentle heat

6 fresh young corn cobs
100 g (3½ oz) demi-sel (lightly salted) butter
1 tablespoon ground piment d'Espelette
 (or hot paprika)
salt and pepper

Strip the husks off the corn cobs. Plunge them into boiling water and cook them for 5 minutes at a bare simmer. Melt half of the butter. Brush the corn with the butter and cook them over gentle heat for 5 minutes, turning them regularly. Serve speared on 2 picks, sprinkle over a little piment d'Espelette, add a pat of butter, season.

VEGETABLES GRILLED WITH MINT

Serves 6
Preparation time 20 minutes
Cooking time 10 minutes on the hotplate

12 spears of green asparagus
1 bunch mint
12 mild green chillies
12 mild red chillies
12 cherry tomatoes
200 g (7 oz/1⅓ cups) fresh peas
100 g (3½ oz/½ cup) fresh broad beans
2 tablespoons olive oil
salt and pepper

Cut the asparagus spears in half lengthways, then into two sections. pick the leaves from the mint. Remove the seeds from the chillies.
On a hotplate that's nice and hot, sauté all the vegetables in the olive oil to sear them (they should stay firm). Add the mint at the end, season.

GRILLED CEP MUSHROOMS

Serves 6
Preparation time 10 minutes + 1 day to find them
Cooking time 5 minutes over high heat

12 small cep mushrooms ('champagne cork' or bouchon)
150 ml (5 fl oz/approx ⅔ cup) olive oil
sea salt and pepper

When the basket is overflowing with cep mushrooms, when the legs are heavy, when the call of the table is felt in the belly and the fangs sharpen, then it is high time to head home and show off the day's pickings.
Scrape the mushrooms with a knife and wipe them. Cut them in half. Pour the olive oil into a small dish. Briefly dip the mushrooms in the oil, cut-side down, sear them over high heat 2 minutes on the cut side and 2 minutes on the outside.
Season with sea salt and pepper.

EGGPLANT GRILLED WITH SAGE

With girls

Serves 6
Preparation time 15 minutes
Cooking time 10 minutes over gentle heat

12 sage leaves, reserve a few for garnish
150 ml (5 fl oz/approx ⅔ cup) olive oil
2 lovely eggplants (aubergines)
sea salt

The night before, process the sage leaves with the olive oil, leave at room temperature. Slice the eggplants into rounds 5 mm (¼ inch) thick. Drizzle the slices of eggplant with the sage oil.
The next day, barbecue the eggplant slices until soft, marking them with a criss-cross grill pattern. Season with sea salt, and garnish with a few sage leaves.

RATATOUILLE PARCELS

With different girls

Serves 6
Preparation time 15 minutes
Cooking time 15 minutes over gentle heat

2 beautiful eggplants (aubergines)
2 red capsicums (peppers)
2 yellow capsicums (peppers)
4 bulb spring onions
50 g (1¾ oz) fresh ginger
1 organic lemon (unwaxed)
150 ml (5 fl oz/approx ⅔ cup) olive oil
100 ml (3½ fl oz/approx ½ cup) white port
1 branch rosemary
1 bay leaf
salt and pepper

Finely dice the vegetables. Peel and finely slice the ginger,
cut the lemon into segments.
Make a parcel by layering two sheets of foil. Place all of the
vegetables inside the parcel, add the ginger, olive oil, port,
rosemary, bay leaf and lemon, season, seal tightly.
Cook over gentle heat for 15 minutes.

GRILLED FENNEL AND ZUCCHINI

Serves 6
Preparation time 15 minutes
Cooking time 10 minutes on the hotplate

3 young zucchinis (courgettes)
3 fennel bulbs
3 red onions
1 bird's eye chilli
1 sprig rosemary
1 sprig fresh thyme
2 tablespoons soy sauce
2 tablespoons olive oil
salt and pepper

Slice the zucchini into thin strips, removing the seeds in
the middle. Peel and slice the fennel bulbs and onions.
Finely chop the chilli, making sure you remove the seeds.
Sear everything in the olive oil on the hotplate, add the
thyme and rosemary, cook 10 minutes. Deglaze with the
soy sauce, season.

AGED COMTÉ BROCHETTES

Serves 6
Preparation time 30 minutes
Freezing time 15 minutes
Cooking time 5 minutes on the hotplate

200 g (7 oz) aged Comté cheese (or gruyére)
50 g (1¾ oz/⅓ cup) sesame seeds
2 stale slices brioche
1 teaspoon sichuan peppercorns
2 eggs
100 ml (3½ fl oz/approx ½ cup) olive oil
1 sprig fresh thyme

Cut the Comté cheese into 2 cm cubes. Process together the sesame seeds, brioche and sichuan peppercorns. Whisk the eggs together with a fork. Dip the cubes of cheese in the beaten egg, then in the crumb mixture, place in the freezer for 15 minutes and repeat this process. Cook the cubes on the hotplate in olive oil on all sides until golden brown, skewer with a toothpick, serve with some tips of thyme.

CRUMBED MOZZARELLA

Serves 6
Preparation time 30 minutes
Freezing time 20 minutes
Cooking time 7 to 8 minutes on the hotplate

100 g (3½ oz/⅔ cup) blanched pistachios
1 biscotte (slice of toasted bread)
1 teaspoon pepper
1 teaspoon dried thyme
3 balls of buffalo mozzarella
2 eggs
olive oil
sea salt

Process the pistachios with the biscotte, pepper and thyme. Take the balls of mozzarella out of their packaging and place them in the freezer for 15 minutes. Whisk the eggs together with a fork. Dip the mozzarella balls in the eggs then roll them in the pistachio crumbs, place them in the freezer for a further 5 minutes. Cook the mozzarella balls on the hotplate for 3–4 minutes then turn them over for a further 3–4 minutes. Place them in a small bowl, drizzle with a little olive oil and season with sea salt.

CAMEMBERT

With a cult figure

Serves 6
Preparation time 10 minutes
Freezing time 10 minutes
Cooking time 10 minutes over gentle heat

2 camemberts in wooden boxes (preferably
  from Normandy)
50 ml (approx 1¾ fl oz/3 tablespoons) calvados
herb assortment

Take the camemberts out of their wooden boxes. Soak the boxes in cold salted water for 10 minutes. Place the camemberts in the freezer for 10 minutes. Carefully cut a thin 'lid' off the top of the camembert, make incisions in the camemberts with a knife, sprinkle with calvados, scatter with herbs and replace the lid. Place the camemberts back into their boxes, wrap in foil and cook over gentle heat for 10 minutes.

Drink with: a red. Camembert has the ability to elevate the simplest red wine

ALMOND-CRUSTED GOAT'S CHEESE

Serves 6
Preparation time 10 minutes
Freezing time 15 minutes
Cooking time 5 minutes on the hotplate

6 firm goat's cheeses (preferably
  rocamadour cheeses)
100 g (3½ oz/approx 1 cup) flaked almonds
2 tablespoons liquid honey
1 tablespoon herbes de Provence (usually
  marjoram, oregano, rosemary, thyme)
coarsely ground black pepper
olive oil

Dip the cheeses in the honey, then in the flaked almonds,
making sure they stick well to the cheese. Sprinkle with
herbes de Provence and black pepper. Place in the freezer
for 15 minutes.
Sear the goat's cheeses, almond-side down, in the olive oil
on the hotplate for 2 minutes, turn them using a spatula
and finish cooking for 2 minutes on the other side.

PICODONS WITH ROSEMARY

With a cheese maker who's also rearing a pig

Serves 6
Preparation time 10 minutes
Cooking time 10 minutes over gentle heat, covered

18 very thin slices of speck (smoked ham or bacon)
6 matured goat's cheeses (preferably picodon cheeses)
6 sprigs rosemary

Arrange the slices of speck two by two in the shape of
a cross, place one cheese in the middle of each. Close up
like a wallet, hold in place with a sprig rosemary.
Cook over gentle heat 10 minutes, covered.

**Drink with: viognier with a subtle nose of apricot tart and
honey**

APPLES AND ROQUEFORT IN BRIK PASTRY

Serves 6
Preparation time 15 minutes
Cooking time 5 minutes on the hotplate

300 g (10½ oz) roquefort cheese
2 granny smith apples
50 g (1¾ oz/approx ⅓ cup) walnuts
1 egg
6 sheets of brik pastry (or filo pastry—see Note)
1 handful rocket
olive oil

Cut the roquefort cheese into thin slivers. Peel the apples,
halve them, remove the core and slice. Roughly chop the
walnuts. Lightly whisk the egg. Lay the roquefort cheese on
the sheets of brik pastry, scatter with walnuts, add the apples
and the rocket. Close to make a turnover, seal the edges with
egg. Cook the brik parcels on the hotplate in olive oil until
golden brown, 2–3 minutes each side.

Note: Brik is a Tunisian dish of pastry wrapped around food
and fried. Brik pastry is purchased in packages of rounds. It is
often called Malsouka and can be found in specialist food
stores. Filo pastry is an ideal substitute. Large Chinese round
won ton wrappers are also similar.

THE BITS ON THE SIDE

APPLES AND GINGER

With your intended, you need to make sure!!!

Serves 6
Preparation time 30 minutes
Cooking time 10 minutes on the hotplate

6 reine des reinettes apples (pippins)
juice of 2 lemons
2 tablespoons rum
3 tablespoons sultanas
30 g (1 oz) fresh ginger
50 g (1¾ oz/approx ⅓ stick) demi-sel
  (lightly salted) butter
3 tablespoons caster (superfine) sugar
3 tablespoons blanched pistachios
2 tablespoons blanched almonds

Peel the apples, remove the core, cut them into segments, sprinkle them with lemon juice.
Heat the rum with 100 ml (3½ fl oz/approx ½ cup) water, add the sultanas. Peel and cut the ginger into thin matchsticks.
Melt the butter on the hotplate, add the apples and the ginger, cook for 5 minutes. Add the sugar, drained sultanas (reserve the liquid), pistachios and almonds, cook for a further 5 minutes. Deglaze with the sultana water. Serve hot.

Drink with: vodka ginger cocktail, you need to forget!

BANANA FLAMBÉE

With the in-laws

Serves 6
Preparation time 5 minutes
Cooking time 10 minutes over gentle heat

1 vanilla bean
500 ml (17 fl oz/2 cups) rum
6 ripe bananas
6 tablespoons sugar

The night before, split the vanilla bean in two and scrape out the seeds, and macerate the bean and seeds in the rum.
Place the bananas on the barbecue, cook 5 minutes on each side (the skin will blacken and start to split).
Heat 200 ml (7 fl oz/approx ¾ cup) of the vanilla rum on the barbecue, flambé.
On each plate, open up the banana skin, sprinkle with sugar and flambéd rum.

Drink with: the rest of the vanilla rum over 2 ice cubes

APPLE WITH ALMOND CREAM

With the children and their friends

Serves 6
Preparation time 20 minutes
Cooking time 15 minutes over gentle heat

30 g (1 oz/approx ⅓ cup) ground almonds
30 g (1 oz/2 tablespoons) sugar
1 egg
6 granny smith apples
30 g + 60 g (1 oz + 2¼ oz) butter
600 ml (21 fl oz/approx 2½ cups) cider

Melt 30 g (1 oz) butter, combine it with the ground almonds, sugar and egg. Put the whole mixture into a piping bag.
Peel the apples, core them whole, fill with the almond cream.
Make six foil parcels, divide the 60 g (2¼ oz) butter between each one and the cider. Place an apple in each parcel and seal tightly, cook over gentle heat 15 minutes.

Drink with: the same cider, well chilled

THE BITS ON THE SIDE

MIRABELLE PLUM

With your nanna because she likes sweet things

Serves 6
Preparation time 10 minutes
Cooking time 15 minutes over gentle heat

600 g (1 lb 5 oz) Mirabelle
(small yellow) plums
500 ml (17 fl oz/2 cups) muscat
3 tablespoons chestnut honey
60 g (2¼ oz) butter
6 sprigs lemon thyme
300 ml (10½ fl oz/approx 1¼ cups) thick cream
60 g (2¼ oz/approx ¼ cup) caster (superfine) sugar

Make six foil parcels and divide the plums between them. Combine the muscat with the honey, sprinkle the plums with this mixture, add some butter and lemon thyme. Seal the parcels tightly, cook over gentle heat for 15 minutes. Whip the cream to soft peaks, add the sugar. Open the parcels, discard the lemon thyme, add a generous tablespoon of chantilly cream. Serve immediately.

Drink with: round, rich and sweet muscat

FRUIT SKEWERS WITH COCONUT MILK POWDER

With Joséphine, Marie-Christine…

Serves 6
Preparation time 15 minutes
Cooking time 10 minutes over gentle heat

1 pineapple
2 mangoes
2 tablespoons rum
2 tablespoons honey
3 tablespoons coconut milk powder

Peel the pineapple, remove the 'eyes', cut into six segments and remove the core. Cut the pineapple segments into slices 1 cm (½ inch) thick. Peel the mangoes, cut them into pieces the same size as the slices of pineapple. Thread them onto skewers, alternating pineapple and mango.
Combine the honey and rum, brush the skewers with this mixture, sprinkle with coconut milk powder. Cook over gentle heat for 10 minutes. The fruits should caramelise.

Drink with: Planter's Punch

APRICOT AND ROSEMARY SKEWERS

With the neo-eco-bio-cool. We'll pick our own apricots, cut some rosemary from the garden, a little organic honey…

Serves 6
Preparation time 15 minutes
Cooking time 5 minutes over high heat

18 apricots
12 stalks of rosemary
Orange syrup:
3 tablespoons honey
juice of 1 orange
50 g (1¾ oz) demi-sel (lightly salted) butter
100 ml (3½ fl oz/approx ½ cup) peach liqueur

Cut the apricots in two, spear them on the stalks of rosemary, making them overlap.
For the syrup, combine the honey with the orange juice, reduce in a saucepan, add the butter and the peach liqueur, reduce again: the texture should be syrupy.
Cook the apricot skewers over high heat for 5 minutes. Serve immediately, coated with syrup.

Drink with: non-vintage fizzy or a luscious sweet chenin blanc

APPENDICES

BL
OOP
ERS
& DIY BARBECUE

BARBECUE BLOOPERS

1- My wood isn't dry enough—it's a free Turkish
bath for cow, calf and consort.
2- I get clever with the rotisserie—a fight breaks out.
3- I revive the barbecue with methylated spirits…
is something burning?
4- My coals are too hot, or is it the 'raw-burnt' diet?
5- I prepare a barbecue in midsummer in a high
wind, and replant a forest the following year…

Come and get it while it's hot!

THE HIGH-TECH BARBECUE

1- The barbecutheque
2- UV lamp so you can still tan at night
3- Wood chopping block to keep grandpa happy
4- Carving board in case you have to share the beef rib cutlet…
5- Silver sauceboat from grandma's dinner service (have to keep her happy too)
6- Extinguisher…of thirst. That's funny, it's spraying rosé!
7- Supercar dashboard, turbo-charged (stainless steel design)
8- Barbecue FM set to "sausage.7 MHz"
9- Organic pantry, in case there's not enough meat
10- All-terrain 15 cm (6 inch) wheels

THE BARBECUE OF THE LONE FISHERMAN

THE INGREDIENTS:
a windproof firelighter
(it gets gusty by the
seaside)

dead leaves
(if they're not all gone
with the wind)

some twigs, nice and dry

some driftwood (keep the
best-looking piece to make
a lamp base)

1 Dig a hole in the sand and surround with rocks.

2 Place the dead leaves in the bottom, without packing them too tight.

3

4 Then arrange the twigs and cross the pieces of driftwood crossed. Make sure the air can circulate.

5 Light the dead leaves at the bottom of the pile to make a big flame

6 Let your wood burn until you get some lovely embers.

If you haven't found anything to make a barbecure grill, your fishing rod will do the job.

Note: Be aware of fire restrictions in all areas as well as restrictions on the collection of firewood.

HOTPLATE BLOOPERS

1- I forgot to clean my hotplate, the beef will be doing its best sardine impression.
2- My hotplate isn't hot enough, it looks like a tableau of burned food.
3- Not having checked the gas level on Saturday, I have no choice but to improvise on Sunday.
4- I cook under a tree, it's guano sauce for lunch.

INDEX

INDEX BY RECIPE

A
Aged Comté Brochettes 230
Almond-Crusted Goat's Cheese 234
Anchovies on Toast 182
Andouillette en Papillote 126
Apple with Almond Cream 238
Apples and Ginger 238
Apples and Roquefort in Brik Pastry 234
Apricot and Rosemary Skewers 242

B
Banana Flambée 238
Basic Mayonnaise 22
Basil Lamb Skewers 50
Bass with Fennel 170
Basting 16
Béarnaise 24
Beef and Prawns Skewers 38
Beef Comté Yakitori 76
Beef Rib Cutlet 142
Beef Shoulder Marinated in Canola Oil 102
Beef with Apples and Spices Skewers 42
Beef with Figs and Sake Skewers 38
Beurre Blanc 24
Black Seabream 172
Bollywood Skewers 46
Boned Saddle of Rabbit 104
Breakfast Burger 134
Butterflied Lamb Shoulder 116

C
Caillettes 86
Cajun-Style Chicken 160
Camembert 230
Capsicum + Chorizo 218
Chicken Breast with Coconut Milk 94
Chicken Burger 132
Chicken Heart Skewers 60
Chicken Yakitori 76
Chorizo Omelette 134
Classic Burger 130
Cocktail Mayonnaise 22
Corn 218
Creamy Sauces 26
Crumbed Mozzarella 230
Curry Salt 18
Customised Merguez 90
Cuttlefish 186

D
Duck Breast & Zucchini Tournedos 110
Duck Breast Yakitori 76
Duck Tenderloins à L'Orange 98
Duck Tenderloins with Summer Vegetables 98

E
Éclade 208
Eggplant Grilled with Sage 222
Emmanuel's Special Cutlets 148
Emulsion Sauces 24
Epigrams of Lamb with Tamarind 102
Executed Lobster 190
Exotic Sausages 84

F
Far West Ribs 144
Fish Skewers 64
Fish Yakitori 74
Foie Gras Burger 132
Fruit Skewers with Coconut Milk Powder 242

G
Garlic and Chilli Chicken Skewers 46
Garlic Mayonnaise 22
Garlic-Studded Lamb Leg Steak 116
Goat's Cheese Sausages 84
Grilled Cep Mushrooms To Go with a Good Piece of Meat 222
Grilled Fennel and Zucchini 226

H
Hake Yakitori 74
Ham Burger 132
Herb Mayonnaise 22
Hollandaise 24
Home-Made Sausages 84
Honey Pork Skewers 34
Hot Dog 134

J
John Dory 174

K
Kidneys On Licorice 60
King Prawns and Spring Vegetables 194
King Prawns with Fennel 190

L
Lamb, Cumin and Almonds Skewers
Lemon Salmon Skewers 70
Like A Paupiette with Sweet Onions 108

M
Mackerel with Lemon 176
Massaman Lamb Skewers 50
Mayonnaise and its Variations 22
Meat Yakitori 76
Meatballs with Coriander Skewers 42
Mediterranean Sausages 84
Mirabelle Plum 242
Monkfish and Chorizo Skewers 66

O
Olive-Basil Salmon 70
Onglet Kebabs 42
Onions with Pepper Butter 214

P
Pepper Sauce 26
Peppered Calf's Liver 62
Peppermint Lamb Leg Steak 116
Picodons with Rosemary 234
Pineapple Chicken Skewers 46
Pistachio Pesto 212
Pork Chop with Herbs 148
Pork Fillets with Pistachio Pesto 106
Pork Steaks & Wholegrain Mustard 148
Pork with Dried Fruit Skewers 34
Potatoes in Embers 212
Prawns Yakitori 74
Provençal Salt 18

R
Rabbit Thighs with Sundried Tomatoes 102
Rack of Lamb with Tapenade 150
Ratatouille Parcels 224
Razor Clams with Tarragon Butter 204
Red Mullet Liver Toasts 180
Roast Monkfish 198
Roast Salmon 196
Roquefort Sauce 26
Rosemary-Skewered Monkfish 66

S
Saddle of Lamb 118
Saffron Sauce 26
Salmon on Fir 200

Salmon Sauce Verte 186
Salmon Yakitori 74
Salt Rubs 18
Sandwich-Style Duck Breast 124
Sardines 178
Sauce Vierge 212
Sausage in the Embers 90
Scallops and Speck 194
Scallops with Grilled Lettuce 194
Scallops Yakitori 74
Schnitzel and Aged Comté 122
Sesame Salmon Skewers 70
Shallot-Lime Yellowfin Tuna 186
Sichuan Salt 18
Snail-Style Skewers 54
Sorrel Sauce 26
Speck 122
Spiced Tomatoes 212
Spicy Salt 18
Spit-Roasted Lamb 164
Spit-Roasted Suckling Pig 162
Steak with Shiso Skewers 38
Sweet-Sour Chicken Drumsticks 98

T
Tarragon Cream 212
Tarragon Squid 190
The Classic: Heart, Liver, Kidney Skewers 56
The Ground Dwellers 206
'Toaded' Chicken with Mustard 158
Tomatoes with Lemon Thyme 218
Turkish Kebab 134

V
Veal and Ginger Skewers 54
Veal Chops with Shallot Butter 152
Veal Fillet with Streaky Speck Skewers 34
Veal Flank and Sarassou 122
Veal Roulade with Jamón 112
Veal Sweetbread Skewers 60
Veal Yakitori 76
Vegetables Grilled with Mint 222
Vegetarian Burgers 135

W
Wholegrain Mustard Mayonnaise 22

Y
Young Garlic 214

INDEX BY MAJOR INGREDIENT

Almonds
Lamb, Cumin and Almonds 50

Anchovies
Anchovies on Toast 182

Apples
Apple with Almond Cream 238
Apples and Ginger 238
Apples and Roquefort in Brik Pastry 234
Beef with Apples and Spices 42

Apricots
Apricot and Rosemary Skewers 242

Asparagus
Vegetarian Burgers 136
Vegetables Grilled with Mint 222

Banana
Banana Flambée 238

Beef
Back from the Woods Sausages 84
Beef and Prawns 38
Beef Comté Yakitori 76
Beef Rib Cutlet 142
Beef Shoulder Marinated in Canola Oil 102
Beef with Apples and Spices 42
Beef with Figs and Sake 38
Caillettes 84
Classic Burger 130
Customised Merguez 90
Egg Burger 132
Exotic Sausages 85
Goat's Cheese Sausages 84
Meatballs with Coriander 42
Mediterranean Sausages 84
Onglet Kebabs 42
Peppered Calf's Liver
Sausage in the Embers 88
Steak with Shiso 38
The Classic: Heart, Liver, Kidney 56

Bacon
Breakfast Burger 134

Bass
Bass with Fennel 170

Butter
Béarnaise 24
Buerre Blanc 24
Hollandaise 24

Capsicum (Pepper)
Capsicum + Chorizo 218
Ratatouille Parcels 224

Cheese
Aged Comté Brochettes 230
Almond-Crusted Goat's Cheese 234
Apples and Roquefort in Brik Pastry 234
Beef Comté Yakitori 76
Cajun-Style Chicken 160
Camembert 230
Chicken Burger 132
Classic Burger 130
Crumbed Mozzarella 230
Ham Burger 132
Picodons with Rosemary 234
Pistachio Pesto 212
Pork Fillets with Pistachio Pesto 106
Roquefort Sauce 26
Sandwich-Style Duck Breast 125
Schnitzel and Aged Comté 122
Vegetarian Burgers 136
Vegetarian Burgers 136

Chicken
Bollywood 46
Cajun-Style Chicken 160
Chicken Breast with Coconut Milk 94
Chicken Burger 132
Chicken Heart Skewers 60
Chicken Yakitori 76
Garlic and Chilli Chicken 46
Pineapple Chicken 46
Sweet-Sour Chicken Drumsticks 98
'Toaded' Chicken with Mustard 158

Chorizo
Capsicum + Chorizo 218
Chorizo Omelette 134
Monkfish and Chorizo 66

Clams
The Ground-Dwellers 206

Corn
Corn 218

Cream
Pepper Sauce 26
Roquefort Sauce 26
Saffron Sauce 26
Sorrel Sauce 26

Cuttlefish
Cuttlefish 186

Dried Fruit
Pork with Dried Fruit 34

Duck
Duck Breast & Zucchini Tournedos 110
Duck Breast Yakitori 76
Duck Tenderloins a L'Orange 98
Duck Tenderloins with Summer Vegetables 98
Foie Gras Burger 132
Onglet Kebabs 42
Sandwich-Style Duck Breast 124

Eggplant (Aubergine)
Eggplant Grilled with Sage 222
Ratatouille Parcels 224

Eggs
Béarnaise 24
Buerre Blanc 24
Chorizo Omelette 134
Egg Burger 132
Hollandaise 24

Fennel
Grilled Fennel and Zucchini 226

Figs
Beef with Figs and Sake 38

Foie Gras
Foie Gras Burger 132

Garlic
Young Garlic 214

Hake
Hake Yakitori 74

Ham
Veal Roulade with Jamon 112

Heart
Chicken Heart Skewers 60
The Classic: Heart, Liver, Kidney 56

John Dory
John Dory 174

Lamb
Basil Lamb 50
Butterflied Lamb Shoulder 116
Emmanuel's Special Cutlets 148
Epigrams of Lamb with Tamarind 102
Garlic-Studded Lamb Leg Steak 116
Lamb, Cumin and Almonds 50
Massaman Lamb 50
Peppermint Lamb Leg Stead 116
Rack of Lamb with Tapenade 150
Saddle of Lamb 118
Spit-Roasted Lamb 164
Turkish Kebab 134

Liver
Peppered Calf's Liver 62
The Classic: Heart, Liver, Kidney 56

Lobster
Executed Lobster 190

Mackerel
Mackerel with Lemon 176

Mangoes
Fruit Skewers with Coconut Milk
Powder 242

Monkfish
Monkfish and Chorizo 66
Roast Monkfish 198
Rosemary-Skewered Monkfish 66

Mullet
Red Mullet Liver Toasts 180

Mushrooms
Grilled Cep Mushrooms to go
with a Good Piece of Meat 222
Onglet Kebabs 42
Veal and Ginger Skewers 54
Veal Sweetbread Skewers 60

Mussels
Éclade 208
The Ground-Dwellers 206

Oil
Basic Mayonnaise 22
Cocktail Mayonnaise 22

Garlic Mayonnaise 22
Herb Mayonnaise 22
Wholegrain Mustard Mayonnaise 22

Onions
Onions with Pepper Butter 214

Oysters
The Ground-Dwellers 206

Pineapple
Fruit Skewers with Coconut Milk
Powder 242
Pineapple Chicken Skewers 46

Plums
Mirabelle Plum 242

Pork
Andouillette en Papillote 126
Far West Ribs 144
Ham Burger 132
Honey Pork 34
Hot Dog 134
Pork Chop with Herbs 148
Pork Fillets with Pistachio Pesto 106
Pork Steaks & Wholegrain Mustard 148
Pork with Dried Fruit 34
Spit-Roasted Suckling Pig 162

Potatoes
Potatoes in Embers 212

Prawns
Beef and Prawns 38
King Prawns and Spring Vegetables 194
King Prawns with Fennel 190
Prawns Yakitori 74

Rabbit
Boned Saddle of Rabbit 104
Rabbit Thighs with Sundried
Tomatoes 102

Razor Clams
Razor Clams with Tarragon Butter 204
The Ground-Dwellers 206

Salt
Curry Salt 18
Provençal salt 18
Sichuan Salt 18
Spicy Salt 18

Salmon
Lemon Salmon 70
Olive-Basil Salmon 70

Roast Salmon 196
Salmon on Fir 200
Salmon Sauce Verte 186
Salmon Yakitori 74
Sesame Salmon 70

Sardines
Sardines 178

Scallops
Scallops and Speck 194
Scallops with Grilled Lettuce 194
Scallops Yakitori 74

Seabream
Black Seabream 172

Speck
Egg Burger 132
Picodons with Rosemary 234
Roast Monkfish 198
Sausage in the Embers 88
Scallops and Speck 194
Speck 122
Veal Fillet with Streaky Speck 34

Squid
Tarragon Squid 190

Tomatoes
Sauce Vierge 212
Spiced Tomatoes 212
Tomatoes with Lemon Thyme 218
Vegetables Grilled with Mint 222

Tuna
Shallot-Lime Yellowfin Tuna 186

Veal
Kidneys on Licorice 60
Like a Paupiette with Sweet Onions 108
Schnitzel and Aged Comté 122
Snail-Style Skewers 54
The Classic: Heart, Liver, Kidney 56
Veal and Ginger Skewers 54
Veal Chops with Shallot Butter 152
Veal Fillet with Streaky Speck 34
Veal Flank and Sarassou 122
Veal Roulade with Jamon 112
Veal Sweetbread Skewers 60
Veal Yakitori 76

Zucchini (Courgette)
Grilled Fennel and Zucchini 226

First published in France in 2011 by Marabout (Hachette Livre)
This edition published in Australia in 2011 by Murdoch Books Pty Limited

Murdoch Books Australia
Pier 8/9, 23 Hickson Road
Millers Point NSW 2000
Phone: +61 (0)2 8220 2000
Fax: +61 (0)2 8220 2558
www.murdochbooks.com.au
info@murdochbooks.com.au

Murdoch Books UK Limited
Erico House, 6th Floor
93–99 Upper Richmond Road
Putney, London SW15 2TG
Phone: +44 (0) 20 8785 5995
Fax: +44 (0) 20 8785 5985
www.murdochbooks.co.uk
info@murdochbooks.co.uk

For Corporate Orders & Custom Publishing contact Noel Hammond,
National Business Development Manager

Photography: Marie-Pierre Morel
Illustrations: José Reis de Matos
Graphic design: Anne Martiréné
Copy-editing: Natacha Kotchetkova and Véronique Dussidour

Project manager: Laura Wilson
English translation: Melissa McMahon
Editor: Carol Jacobson
Production: Joan Beal

National Library of Australia Cataloguing-in-Publication entry

Author: Reynaud, Stéphane.
Title: Stéphane Reynaud's BBQ / Stéphane Reynaud.
ISBN: 978-1-74266-240-4 (pbk.)
Subjects: Barbecuing, Cooking.
Dewey Number: 641.5784

Printed by 1010 Printing International Limited, China.

IMPORTANT: Those who might be at risk from the effects of salmonella poisoning
(the elderly, pregnant women, young children and those suffering from immune deficiency
diseases) should consult their doctor with any concerns about eating raw eggs.

OVEN GUIDE: You may find cooking times vary depending on the oven you are using.
For fan-forced ovens, as a general rule, set the oven temperature to 20°C (35°F) lower
than indicated in the recipe.